George W. Bailey

A Private Chapter of the War

1861-5.

George W. Bailey

A Private Chapter of the War
1861-5.

ISBN/EAN: 9783744747929

Printed in Europe, USA, Canada, Australia, Japan

Cover: Foto ©ninafisch / pixelio.de

More available books at **www.hansebooks.com**

1864.

A Private Chapter of the War.

(1861-5.)

BY

GEO. W. BAILEY,

Late First Lieut. 6th Mo. Infty., and A.D.C. 2d Div. Staff, 15th Army Corps.

ST. LOUIS:
G. I. JONES AND COMPANY.
1880.

DEDICATORY.

TO

MRS. CARRIE E. HAMBRICK,

Of Atlanta, Ga., whose nobility of soul manifested itself in rising above surrounding prejudices and circumstances, proving superior to them, by extending welcome and bestowing aid and comfort upon a helpless *stranger* whom the misfortunes of war brought to her door, and whose life was preserved by her motherly care, sympathy, and encouragement, this volume is respectfully dedicated by

THE AUTHOR.

INTRODUCTORY.

This volume is not a complete history of military experiences of the writer; if so, it would necessarily embrace a period of time extending between September, 1861, and April, 1865. It would include enlistment and fifteen months' service as a private soldier in the Sixth Infantry, Connecticut Volunteers, Army of the Potomac, at Washington; the ocean trip from Fortress Monroe to Port Royal, South Carolina, and the picturesque bombardment and reduction, at the latter place, of Forts Walker and Beauregard, November 7, 1861, and the first lodgment of Union forces on South Carolina soil; the campaign and expeditions about Hilton Head and Beaufort, South Carolina, down to February, 1863; the promotion and transfer to the Sixth Infantry, Missouri Volunteers, Army of the Tennessee; the entire campaign of Vicksburg, with its bloody charges; the Chattanooga campaign, and bloody Mission Ridge; the march to the relief of Gen. Burnside at Knoxville; the Atlanta campaign, with its principal battles and flank movements, in all of which the writer participated either as a private or as an officer with his company, or as A. D. C., Second Division Staff of the Fifteenth Army Corps, and during which he was twice wounded. To embrace these experiences, however interesting, would be foreign to the object of this volume, which is to select from the whole military history a "private chapter," and present it as worthy of being recorded as *uncommon* experiences. It presents a limited inside view of a portion of the Confederacy within its military lines, as secretly observed by a "stray" from the invading army in blue, whose experiences disclose the real political sentiments of fair samples of different classes who resided within the Confederacy during the war,—experiences, not of a spy, not of a scout, but of a harmless escaped prisoner of war,— a refugee; free, yet practically imprisoned; escaped, yet practically confined within broader limits only; guilty of no offence but that of performance of duty in resorting to all proper means and expedients, and promptly taking advantage of all circumstances and occasions, in determined and persistent efforts to regain the Federal lines.

The scene of "operations" lies within a radius of fifty miles south and east of Atlanta, Georgia. The narrative embraces: A description of the battle of Atlanta, July 22, 1864, where Gen. McPherson fell and the writer was captured— Four days only of captivity— Novel means of escape by burial, to avoid Andersonville prison-pen— Two and a half months secreted in the woods and forests of Georgia— Varied experiences among rich and poor, whites and blacks— Frequent narrow escapes from recapture by Confederate cavalry —Desperate, unsuccessful efforts to reach the Federal lines— Conflicting and confusing reports of Gen. Sherman's defeat and retreat from Atlanta — Excitement caused by the announcement, "Atlanta's taken!" — The final desperate attempt of the writer, armed, to reach the Federal lines— Successful and perilous approach to a point six miles east of Atlanta, and *one mile* from Federal pickets — Singular recapture by two guerrillas, one in butternut, the other a *decoy* in blue, whose names are given, and whose "business" it was to "muster out" unarmed Federal prisoners — The promise to treat the captive as a "prisoner of war" — Conducting the writer into thick woods under a false pretence, and there announcing to him, "*This is as good a place to die as any man could wish*"— The "two minutes" accorded for prayer—

Frivolous pretexts for the attempted murder — The interesting conversation that followed the announcement — The *ruse* — The sudden flight for life — The shooting four times at the captive, one shot taking effect with almost fatal result — The marvellous escape — A ghastly wound — The kind care and sympathy of white ladies, who are introduced to the reader — Information secretly conveyed to the Federal lines by night — Prompt response of "Garrard's New York cavalry," U. S. V., one hundred and fifty strong, with ambulance and surgeon — The wounded and helpless writer conveyed to the Federal lines at Atlanta — The wound pronounced "mortal" — Slow and tedious recovery — Governmental recognition of duty performed — Revisitation, in 1870, of the scenes and friends of 1864, together with portraits of the principal persons referred to in this "chapter."

The writer is aware that many of the incidents related may not seem plausible, and will tend to create incredulity, especially among those who do not wish to believe. In recognition of this tendency, the names and residences of other living witnesses are given.

The writer is in possession of additional evidences not available for the press, — bullet-scarred body, bullet-torn coat, stiffened with his blood, maps, compass, cartridges, and numerous other relics of his experience, — which are subject to the inspection of the incredulous or curious.

Let the reader consider for a moment the probable percentage of those who were conducted to secluded places for the purpose of being "mustered out" in cold blood, for the "crime" of wearing the Federal uniform, who escaped to relate the unenviable experience. Such contemplation will doubtless lead most readers to agree that it devolves upon the writer, as a solemn duty, to present this volume to the public, comprising, as he does, the small percentage of *one* among — HOW MANY!

INTRODUCTORY.

How many books will be written, how many confessions made, by those who participated on the *safe* side of such experiences?

How many are there, who were not on the preferred side of similar experiences, and who would be *willing* witnesses thereof, who were not *stricken dumb* at the time, and ever after remained silent?

Surely, one of so rare experience should not hesitate to move tongue and pen, as constituting the *surviving percentage* among an unknown number of victims, and present not only facts, but names and portraits of those connected therewith, as is done in this volume.

In the relation of the bloody work of outlaws, no reflections are intended upon soldiers who wore the gray uniform in honorable warfare. Infamous conduct, unmasking fiends, will ever meet the condemnation of all civilized persons, and especially of all *soldiers*, irrespective of the color of the uniforms disgraced by assassins.

In explanation of the delay in publication, it is sufficient to state that, for the reasons herein indicated, earlier publication was considered detrimental to the interests of some of the principal "witnesses" residing in Georgia.

GEO. W. BAILEY.

ST. LOUIS, May, 1880.

A PRIVATE CHAPTER OF THE WAR.

July 22, 1864; before Atlanta, Ga.—Early this morning, our pickets reported that the enemy in our front (Army of the Tennessee) had retired from the intrenched position occupied yesterday. Our skirmishers were pushed forward into the abandoned Confederate works. This had been the eastern line of defence, and is located about three miles east of Atlanta, extending across the railroad which runs eastward. The writer was aide-de-camp on the staff of Maj. Gen. Morgan L. Smith, and at this time ranking as first lieutenant. Gen. Smith then commanded the Second Division of the Fifteenth Army Corps. This corps, together with the Seventeenth, comprising the Army of the Tennessee, promptly moved up and occupied the abandoned works of the Confederates, and soon reversed them, making them available for means of defence against Confederate advances. The day advanced,—and so did the enemy! Our lines were being extended on the extreme left; and the Seventeenth Corps had hardly arrived at its place in the extension, when away southward, and rather to the rear of the line of the Fifteenth Corps, began suspicious sounds of desultory skirmishing. The sounds grew heavier and heavier, until it was apparent that our lines were either seriously opposed or else being attacked. The sputtering of skirmish-rifles now became a continuous rattle of musketry. Huge volumes of powder-smoke arose above the tree-tops, and the thunder of artillery was added to the conflict. Then we readily understood what we might soon expect in our front. "We are going to have a fight here," said Gen. Smith, as he sat on his horse in rear of our lines, surrounded by his staff. "They are raising the devil on our left, and we'll catch it here soon!" Already the Confederate shells burst in uncomfortable proximity over our heads, causing our horses to prance to such an extent that they were sent to the rear. A shell burst less than fifteen feet overhead. "Spherical case," said the General, as the bullet missiles hissed and whistled among the foliage. "Oh me! oh me!" cried one of our boys, as he held one arm with the other and limped toward the rear. "Dry up! dry up!" ordered the General. "You're not hurt much, or you couldn't bellow like that." The roar of the conflict seems to increase and approach. An ambulance passes. An orderly says, "Gen. McPherson's killed! He's in that ambulance." Every face was sad; but no time now for inquiries. Every thing is excitement, and every eye is strained toward the woods skirting our front. An orderly sent to order in our outposts returned wounded. The others were absent on duty. "Bailey," said the General to the writer, "would you mind ordering in those fellows?" A horse, — a hasty mounting, — a dash over the works, — a dash over the intervening space, — and the order was delivered. The pickets of the outpost were already engaged with the advancing Confederate skirmish-line, and little leaden messengers hissed and whizzed uncomfortably close, cutting through the air and foliage. A recall of pickets, an excited and confused "falling in," and a hasty repairing to our lines, closely followed by the advancing Confederates. Other pickets are coming in rapidly, and the general report is, "They are coming on us heavy!" While some are comparatively cool, others wear panic-stricken countenances, point wildly toward the woods, and huskily exclaim, "Here they come, boys, four and five lines deep!" "They are right on us!" and hastily climb over the works, and seek shelter behind them. Now there follows a death-like stillness. The sounds of battle have suddenly ceased, and there is a calm before the coming tempest. Ominous silence! Every rifle is cocked, every eye gazing across the space intervening between us and the timber. No words spoken, save the encouraging sentences of our officers. "Bailey," said the General to the writer, "please take a position where you can see if they are massed and where they are massed, and report to me, if you can find out." The writer ran to a slight elevation immediately in rear of our works, where he could obtain a view of the whole front, and there stood with eyes riveted on the timber some three hundred yards in front. What suspense! What silent excitement! Here and there among the brave boys in the works were faces pale as death. They could not have been more ghastly had they been reflections of the countenance of the writer. At last there is observable a great commotion in the distant foliage, and emerging from it, three lines deep, in extraordinary order, come the advancing enemy. How beautiful! How regular! A hasty dressing of the lines without halting, a lowering of bayonets, a charge, and cheers that made the welkin ring! There was a conflict between fear and admiration. Their prowess is unquestioned, but their glory is short! Our lines open! Fire leaps from the crest of our works; the deadly roll of musketry is heard continuously amidst the crashes of double-shotted cannon. Angry-hissing rifle-balls rival grape and canister in spreading dismay and death among our gallant enemies. The continuous roar of the battle drowns all other sounds, and mother earth trembles as if convulsed with an earthquake. Through the smoke of battle, the writer could discern confusion and disorder among the Confederates, while the ground was thickly strewn with dead and wounded. A slight recoil, a hasty reformation of two lines in one, hearty cheers, another charge, another bloody repulse! The sullen foe fall back to the timber in hopeless confusion. Confederate batteries brought forward suddenly open from the edge of the timber, and the air seems thickened with exploding shells and grape shot. Now returning to the timber's edge, reinforced, the repulsed infantry open a heavy musketry-fire, and the deadly "minies" cut through the smoky scene by thousands. Shells tear off the limbs of trees, and scream fearfully through the air; while solid shot tear up the earth, sending great clouds of dust skyward. The dense smoke furnishes an excellent screen, which our repulsed enemies are not slow to take advantage of. Under its cover there is a hasty formation of the remnants of the wreck, and preparation made for another assault. A column of Confederates pressed through our lines, through an unguarded cut in the railroad, and opened an inexplicable fire on our boys from the rear. No one seemed to understand the meaning of this new and decidedly disagreeable feature; nor could it be expected that the best troops would withstand such treatment. Bullets madly hissing from the front, bullets spitefully whizzing from the rear; obscuring smoke of battle; cheers of reformed and charging lines; "confusion worse confounded." But the officers still encourage: "Once more, boys!" "Give it to 'em again!" "Aim low, boys!" There is a desultory rattle of musketry-fire from our works, directed at the unseen lines through the smoke. But the living press the living over the dead and dying, and the scattered survivors of the charge seem compelled to seek protection under our works, hugging mother earth for dear life. The aggravating fire from the rear produces its result. Our lines grow thinner and thinner. Now a Confederate battle-flag is waved over our works, within five feet of the writer. "What! and the old Army of the Tennessee?" Such a sight was never witnessed before, and it was never witnessed again. The writer saw the first Confederate that entered our works. He came in on the wagon-road, which was undefended. Then came another; then three, six, twenty; a host rapidly followed, and alas! our works were carried. The victors rapidly load, and fire indiscriminately through the smoke at our retiring blue-coats; but in the confusion and smoke it is difficult to distinguish friend from foe. Capt. Maddox, also of our division staff, had remained during the battle near to the writer, and we frequently conversed during its progress. Escape and safety were now only to be considered. We attempted to glide through the smoke to the rear. Maddox was almost immediately intercepted, while the writer was more fortunate in executing a small flank-movement, and reaching a point well in the rear, where he had tied his horse; was congratulating himself, when advancing from the rear came the victorious Confederates, wild with delight and crazed with intoxicating drink. The railroad cut! that's the explanation; awful dilemma! "Halt! halt! you d—d Yankee ———!" exclaimed a drunken Confederate, bringing his rifle down and bunglingly endeavoring to take aim. "D—n your soul, I'll shoot you anyhow (hic). Haven't killed my Yankee to-day!" The writer saw his opportunity, and grasping the barrel of the weapon, raised it over his head and held it there. In vain did the Confederate endeavor to lower it and release it. He was a powerful fellow, and for once, at least, the writer found an agreeable ally in — whiskey. "Let go of this sword!" said a voice sharply, from behind. A Confederate officer grasped the drawn blade, and wrenched it out of the writer's hand. He seemed flushed only with excitement. "Captain," said the writer, "this drunken man is trying to shoot me after I've surrendered." "No, no," said the officer, to my great relief. "Here, John" (calling a soldier), "take this officer to the rear, and don't let him be harmed nor robbed,—hear?" John nodded assent. Now pours through the opening swarms of Confederates, cheering, howling, cursing, shooting at imaginary or at least unseen enemies through the smoke. During the confusion an incident occurred worthy of mention. A large, burly "blue-coat," apparently a German, was persistently and hotly pursued by a diminutive and highly decorated Confederate officer. He struck the retreating Federal over the head again and again, occasionally examining his new, glittering sword. He was evidently determined to color his blade with Yankee blood. Was he endeavoring to earn promotion? Did he desire honorable mention for gallant conduct in the "face" of the enemy? Or was he meriting the coveted smiles of Atlanta's fair daughters? Perhaps he had solemnly avowed to a fair bestower of the untarnished weapon that its lustre should only be dimmed by the gore of the enemy. The captive was not permitted to witness the upshot of this incident, even had the smoke permitted. "This way," said his guard, and we passed on the road through our works toward Atlanta. The cries and moans of the wounded arose through the thick smoke. Some Federal dead lay stretched in and near our works, but in front of them was an awful scene. The ground for over one hundred yards was thickly strewn with the rebel dead and wounded. Many cries arose for "water;" some were struggling to extricate themselves from tangled heaps of dead, and calling for aid; some were vainly striving to stop the flow of crimson tide gushing from ghastly wounds; many were fitfully gasping their last breath. But the great majority were grim and cold in the strong embrace of death, lying in almost every conceivable position; some were riddled with rifle-balls; some were torn with grape or canister shot, and at not infrequent intervals the bodies were literally heaped together. There were young and old countenances; some distorted, others calm. Stony eyes gazed meaninglessly at us as we picked our way; others stared wildly into space. "My God! look at that sight," said the guard. "Brave fellows," said the writer. "Yes, and in the *right*, too," fairly hissed the guard. The captive was silent. "What?" said the guard, glaring angrily. "I said nothing," replied the captive. "Well, don't you half think so yourself?" inquired the guard. "This is no time for discussion; of course I can't deny what my uniform expresses," pleaded the captive. "D—n your uniform," spitefully hissed the guard. What's that? The screeching of a shell over our heads. *Bang!* and the pieces of the exploded missile hum and whiz through the air. Another, and another. Now they come in pairs. Now the air is thick with them. Rifle-balls hiss through the air thicker and thicker. Now there is a perfect roar of musketry and artillery. The sounds come nearer and nearer, and the heavy smoke rises behind us like an ominous storm-cloud. "They're coming back on us; we must get out of this," said the guard, as we hurried through the timber. There was no rest that night for the Army of the Tennessee, except upon the ground whence it had been temporarily driven. There was a rally, an immediate counter-assault; cheers rent the air: the struggle for the lost works was in progress. "Look, look!" said the guard; and there came the frightened, retreating Confederates, scattered in confusion, every man for himself, driven back in a wild, fleeing mob. On came the blue lines of infantry, just visible through the smoke. The few disposed to resist were speedily swept away before that glorious tide. The stars and stripes never before seemed so glorious as now they float, dimly visible through the smoke of battle, all along the recaptured works. The captive almost forgot his captivity, and exultingly exclaimed: "That's the old Army of the Tennessee. I knew they'd never stay whipped long!" Wild cheers arose from the works; flags flitted fitfully over the scene; the roar of conflict ceased, and the battle of Atlanta was over. History records the result: Total Union loss, 3,521; total Confederate loss, about 8,000 men, 5,000 stand of arms, eighteen stand of colors, and a victory.

"What of success in skirmish or in fray,
If rout and ruin close the day?"

When nearing Atlanta, amidst utter confusion outside of the main entrenchments, the captive ventured the proposition, "I'll give you my watch and silver spurs if you will march off with them, and forget me a few moments." The guard looked wistfully at the proffered treasures, and then, casting a glance at the confused masses of rebels retreating through the woods, said, "You couldn't reach your lines if I did." "Well, I'll take the chances, if you say so," said the captive. "Well, you'd better come on," said the guard, rather firmly; and we emerged from timber into the clearing before the main entrenchments of Atlanta. There floated the Confederate ensigns; there frowned the great guns; and the entrenchments were crested with Confederate gunners and infantry, all peering eagerly toward the scene of the recent battle. Inside Atlanta, prisoners from other parts of the line accumulate. All formed in column, and the march through the city began. The dust was fearful. One of our soldiers, shot through the lower jaw, and speechless, made signs of distress to the writer. "Major, one of our boys is so badly injured that he can hardly march through this dust; he cannot speak, and would like to ride," said the writer, imploringly, to the Confederate major in command. The major turned abruptly in his saddle, looked at the writer sternly, placed his hand on his revolver-handle, and replied, "Get back into the ranks, there d—d quick, or I'll put a ball through your d—d hide." In obeying the polite command, the writer confronted Capt. Maddox. "Well, well," said he, "I thought you were killed." "That's what I thought about you," was the reply, and a hearty "shake" followed. "There's my horse, Maddox," said the writer, pointing at the animal mounted by a rebel soldier. There was my rubber blanket just as it was left, and my sword-scabbard strapped to the grand saddle, a gift from Gen. Smith. "To what base uses are they come at last." An excited rebel soldier amuses the citizen spectators by trailing one of our captured flags in the dust behind his horse, in our front. Bodies of Confederate infantry were moving rapidly toward the Confederate right flank. Women taunted us with, "Ah! boys, you've got into Atlanta at last, haven't you?" Everybody seemed crazed with delight. The troops cheered so lustily while passing us that it seemed irregular, at least, not to take off our hats in acknowledgment of self-appropriated compliments. Men, women, and children gaze at us good-naturedly; but occasionally there are countenances sneering with scorn or pale with hatred. This is among the rabble. The *élite*, especially the fairer sex, extend only the welcome of compressed lips, and eyes scintillating with expressions of hatred. All had evidently heard only of the "great victory." If they heeded the recent rattle of musketry, and the heavy crashes of artillery which caused the earth to tremble beneath their feet, they misinterpreted them to signify the further discomfiture of the "boys in blue." But a "change came o'er the spirit of their dreams:" Sherman's iron grasp encircled doomed Atlanta.

The Union prisoners were all brought to the yard of the Confederate provost-marshal and enrolled as prisoners of war. Among them were Col. R. K. Scott, Sixty-eighth Ohio Infantry, commanding brigade; Col. Warren Shedd, of the Thirtieth Illinois Infantry; Lieut. Col. Wallace, Forty-seventh Ohio Infantry; Lieut. Col. Saunders, Sixteenth Iowa Infantry; Maj. ——, of the Ninety-ninth Indiana Infantry; a major of Gen. Harrow's staff; Capt. Maddox, One Hundred and Sixteenth Illinois Infantry, and of Second Division, Fifteenth Army Corps, staff; and many other officers of lower rank, all belonging to the Army of the Tennessee, — about eighty officers in all, besides a great number of soldiers. It was now twilight. "Fall in, prisoners!" The line was formed. The officers were separated from and preceded the soldiers. As we marched southward, the streets were filled with old men, women, and children; and the many curious expressions and taunts among the non-combatants suggested, in turn, ignorance, prejudice, indifference, joy, and contempt. Our guards, as a rule, meekly bore their honors without compromising their dignity. "We are going to East Point," said one guard. Since most of us hadn't been to "West Point," we could at least visit East Point; and we merrily indulged in perpetrating puns on these two decided extremes of "East Point, West," and "West Point, East."

What a contrast between the exciting scenes of the day and the calm and silence of the night, broken only by the sounds of the dull tramp through the thick dust, the occasional stern commands of the Confederate officers, and the peaceful voices of the night. It is the gentle approach of evening's holy hour that has bid the raging tumult cease, —

"All things are hushed before her, as she throws
O'er earth and sky her mantle of repose."

A halt. Our infantry guards are relieved by cavalry, and the march resumed. The major of the Ninety-ninth Indiana and the writer concoct a plan of escape. The horrors of Andersonville already loom up before us. The plan is, to pass immediately behind the horse of a guard, to be as far as possible from his follower, and trust to the concealment of the shades of night for the rest. An opportunity arrives; we glide silently out of the ranks, and in an instant are safely concealed in the adjoining woods. A rapid walk; a horse in the path, and also a dismounted cavalryman. The snorting and uneasiness of the horse spreads to the rider. "Who goes there?" he bawled, at the top of his voice. No response; dead silence. Will he fire? "You had better get back into the ranks d—d quick, there, or I'll put a slug through ye," said he, approaching us. The major, doubtless wisely acting under the axiom "Discretion's the better part of valor," immediately glided back toward the road, and the writer felt impelled to reluctantly follow the good example. More indifferent concerning our getting in than our getting out, we joined the rear of the column, were detected, and placed under special guard for the remainder of the march.

The evening was very sultry, the roads very dusty, the day's excitement very exhausting, the prisoners very much fatigued. We had not been invited to lunch, and most of us had eaten nothing since morning. The dust was suffocating; hair, eyes, ears, nostrils, throat, lungs, clothes, — every thing covered or smeared with dust. "Water!" cry the sufferers. "Can't we have some water?" No response. The clouds which veiled the sky slowly passed away, and a soft, silvery, misty light fell upon us. In the dim moonlight we observe an occasional glittering of the arms of our guards. But there are no distinctions now in uniforms; we are all of a color. The blue have all been converted into gray; and buttons no longer bright, shoulder-straps no longer brilliant, refuse to reflect the silvery rays. The general hawking has become painful to the ear. There is a depression in the road, and the head of the column enters a pearly stream flowing across it. We hear the splash of the water, and with gladdened eyes observe the precious flood sparkle as it is forded by weary feet. Water! What a boon! "Water," gratefully utter a hundred thirsty throats; but there is no halt. The guards gruffly command, "Forward there! push on there! close up!" As the jaded and thirsty prisoners are hurried through the rippling stream, hats, caps, hands, every thing, are brought into requisition to acquire a few drops of the cooling stream. Canteens are useless, their possessors spending the precious moments in endeavoring to fill themselves. The writer scooped up and eagerly swallowed what he could obtain by handfuls, but was hurried through and on with the others. He was almost tempted to drink and die. Surely death by drowning had lost all of its terrors. So the panting, hungry, jaded prisoners, burning with thirst, were driven through, yet permitted to drink not of the refreshing gift, water, of all desires the greatest! Delicious stream, of which we dare not partake. It will require argument to convince any of those comprised in this particular column of unfortunates that there are many circumstances which can surpass this in unnecessary suffering on the one hand, or in the exhibition of refined cruelty on the other.

Shortly before midnight we arrived at East Point, Georgia, several miles south of Atlanta, and corralled like mules, an angular entrenchment forming two sides of our limits. The general cry was, Water! the desire for which seemed to be doubly increased by the aggravating circumstances at the ford. "For God's sake, colonel, or major, or captain, give us only a little water!" In undue time water — delicious water — was furnished. A new danger presented itself: overdrinking. But there were thirsty beings there, who would drink, and drink, apparently in disregard of, if not inviting, danger. They thought of nothing, heeded nothing, but water; and seemed willing to pay any penalty for their indulgence. No rations. We immediately stretched our tired bodies on the bare earth, and under the comforting cover of the clouds were soon embraced in the soothing arms of slumber. An hour passed; the writer awoke, cold, and stiff in every joint. A brisk walk around the "pen," for exercise and observation. Oho! a double line of guards, eh? and "no conversation with prisoners." Guess I'll not be able to make that anticipated "watch trade" to-night. A quiet return to "bed;" a rolling and tossing restlessly; a gazing into "the dim-lit vault of the sky;" a mental recapitulation of the battle; a wonder if the General came out safe (reckless man!), and if any of our staff were hurt; how the Sixth Missouri stood it, and the general result of the battle. "A thousand to ten" that the Army of the Tennessee is sleeping in those works at the present moment. A half-vision of charging rebels, fluttering battle-flags, roar and smoke of conflict, moans of wounded, and the stars and stripes triumphantly waving through the smoke of battle, and slumber closes the weary eyelids.

July 23. — Hungry — fasted twenty-four hours. Still no rations. We are permitted to trade with the natives; and the officers, now separated from the soldier-prisoners, are trading watches, pocket-books, jewelry, ornaments, money, finger-rings — every possession but life — for cornbread and other edibles. "What will you give for my watch?" asked the writer of a lean, long, cadaverous-looking corn-bread merchant. He looked at the timepiece a moment, and invitingly held out a small loaf (or "pone") of bread. "No, sir!" indignantly responded the writer. "Will you give four loaves for it?" An emphatic shake of the head. "Then I'll wait four days longer for rations," said the writer. Another enterprising genius peddled watermelons. No possibility of trading silver spurs for bread or potatoes, and desiring to make other use of his watch, he obtained for the spurs part of a very tempting watermelon. At evening the long-hoped-for rations arrived. Hunger was not the enemy that thirst had been. A dealing of rations to the representatives of each mess of ten; one coarse meal cracker and a small bit of bacon, one ration. "This is for twenty-four hours." The writer gratefully accepted his "tenth," and proceeded to prepare it for demolition. The bacon, experts say, consists of the "ends," and is very generally suspected. What an advantage in the maxim, "In the midst of arms, the laws are silent." And why? Because otherwise the occupants of these crackers could show superior titles against us, under the statute of limitations. They'd only have to show ten years' possession. Very mouldy. An economical brushing and blowing, and the writer, for one, was on the outside of his rations in a twinkle. Others shut their eyes and feasted. The only remaining consolation concerning the "tenants" was that they got the worst of it. But the "tenants" did not comprise the whole difficulty.

Many a manly struggle resulted in costing a tooth, and paying with nothing but a worm. Those unaffected by the change of diet slept upon the bosom of mother earth, under the spangled covering, during the second night of captivity.

July 24. — Bright and beautiful morning. Stiffened joints the rule; hardship beginning to produce its effect on many; despondency general; frequent muttering of protests; a few countenances cheerful. Hungry; sickness appearing. "Rations! rations!" cry the prisoners. Articles most valuable and longest retained, hardest to part from, now freely traded for something, anything, to eat; but the majority can neither buy nor beg. The day advances; still no rations, no explanation. The clamor for something to eat becomes boisterous; loud expressions of indignation. There is a commotion indicating a spirit of revolt. A battery of Napoleon guns bearing on us are suggestively pointed at by the commanding officer, who sternly advises peaceful submission. Confederate gunners carelessly loll upon and around the guns, with a "ready" appearance. "Double-shotted with canister, eh? Well, we want something to eat, that's all; we can't starve submissively." To those who had so recently witnessed the terrible effect of canister, the brazen muzzles of the frowning guns had a peculiar significance, a soothing effect. Music by the band — brass band. Prisoners regaled by the stirring notes of "The Bonnie Blue Flag," "Dixie," and other "national" airs. [Those notes sound in the writer's memory as if but rendered yesterday.] Especially fine were the cornet variations in "The Bonnie Blue Flag." Toward the middle of the afternoon we were startled by the singing of a hymn near our enclosure. Now a fervent prayer: an invocation of the Divine blessing upon "our glorious army" and "righteous cause;" "the president of these Confederate States, and all of our civil and military authorities;" "our sick and wounded and mourning;" an emphatic "Amen!" What! no word for us? Is that Christian charity? Guess that chaplain has heard of the result of Hood's attempt to drive the Yankees back to Chattanooga. There's considerable human nature in — human nature. There is more charity in the singing; the good old hymns have the same words as at home, and the harmony is fine, the effect soothing. Slumber. Though the body was captive, the spirit was unconfined. It passed the rebel sentries without challenge, flew over contending armies, and dwelt among kind friends and pleasant faces. Harmonious sounds of voices and rich strains of music greeted it; no enemy, no gruff sentries, no hunger, no hardship, no war; peace and plenty. Even the sweet face of one who had recently passed from earthly scenes returned from its better abode to greet it, and again respond to the endearing name of — mother! A sudden shock; an awakening; a drowsy realization of the beautiful delusion; a reluctant appreciation of the situation; slow moving of obstinate limbs; reluctant action of stiffened joints.

Evening. Rations at last; same as before in quality and quantity. We were informed by announcement that these rations were issued in advance for the following twenty-four hours. Useless to protest; we had but one remaining right — the right to submit. "That's the best we can do; we are short of rations for our own troops," said the major. Most of us devoured the "twenty-four hours rations in advance" at one standing. Darkness again; sleep, broken only by the relief of the guards or by the challenges of sentries. Morning.

July 25. — Continued silence in the direction of Atlanta. What was the result of the battle? how many killed? what does this silence mean? has Sherman fallen back? has Hood evacuated? were questions occasionally asked, but no reliable responses elicited. One genius said, "The Yankees can't fight for awhile; all the live ones are busy burying the dead ones." (Astounding announcement — astute sentry!) "How long are we going to be kept in this miserable place?" "How long are we to be kept on quarter-rations?" Nobody seemed to know. We knew that exchanges of prisoners had ceased because of a misunderstanding or disagreement concerning the *status* of negro troops, and that no immediate prospects were entertained that the question could be speedily settled. The gloomy prospect of Andersonville loomed up again. Horrifying contemplation. A careful mental consideration and adjustment of chances for life resulted in favor of a desperate attempt to escape, rather than attempt to survive Andersonville. While thus contemplating, we were startled by the loud, stern command of a Confederate major, ordering, "Fall in, prisoners! Hurry up!" A hasty formation into line (no trouble about baggage), a march southward, the officers separated from the soldier-captives. Where are we going? Don't know; can't ascertain — but toward Andersonville.

Confederate officers rather provoke argument on the subject of the war, and many interesting discussions ensue. No opportunity afforded an invitation to attempt to escape. Near evening we march through Jonesboro, Georgia, some twenty miles south of Atlanta, situated on the Macon Railroad. Inhabitants line the street; first Yankees — great curiosities. Whites rather jubilant; the pitying glances of the blacks indicate their sympathy. Desiring confirmation, an opportunity was sought to converse with a negro. (A beckoning, an approach.) "Stop that," said the guard. "Get back there, you d—d nigger." But the mere prompt effort on the part of the negro to respond was convincing enough of sympathy and friendship. Two miles below the town, and we reach our quarters for the night—open field. A blanket is carelessly thrown among the prisoners, and falls upon the writer. Providential; a great luxury; comforting rest assured. (A few fires; retirement, sharing the precious blanket with a fellow-captive. I wonder, suspect. No—yes; it is not gentle thoughts that "come o'er me stealing." But there's something—a new enemy. Retreat? Impossible; a detachment of the enemy already in possession; vain attempt at dislodgment. And they are ex-Confederates, too! Ravenous. Sleep impossible; escape possible. A guard approached.) "Halt there!" said he. "I want to speak with you a moment," said the prisoner; "I've something interesting to say to you." "Well, what is it?" asked the sentry. "I have a very fine timepiece here (old silver 'turnip'), and if you'll do me a small favor you can have it," said the prisoner. The sentry seemed not averse to possessing the watch; and, looking wistly at it, asked, "What favor do you want for it?" "Turn your back and don't see me pass out," said the prisoner. "Agreed," said the sentry. "I'll be back in a few moments," said the prisoner. (A return to obtain a canteen and beg a little "hardtack;" a whispered "goodbye;" a stealthy reapproach.) "Halt! where are you going?" demanded the sentry. "It's only myself. It's all right," said the prisoner, approaching; "don't speak so loud." "Stop, d—d you!" said the sentry, emphatically, bringing down his rifle. Thunder! A new guard. The clanking sound of an officer's scabbard approached the sentry as the distance lengthened between him and the chagrined captive, who picked his way through the prostrated forms of prisoners back to his "mess" and cast his weary self upon "mother earth" and slept until the early morning of—

July 26, — When we were gruffly ordered to "Fall in, prisoners," and over very dusty roads marched rapidly southward. No rations. At early evening we were corralled in a large enclosure or pasture some ten miles north of Griffin, Georgia, near "Big Sandy Creek." Several beautiful young ladies visited us from a neighboring plantation, and while not compromising themselves, nor their friends who wore the gray, they still seemed to possess those tender natures which sympathized with suffering humanity even in blue, and kindly distributed among the prisoners who approached them royal gifts in the shape of luscious apples, of which the writer was fortunate enough to obtain one. The occasion also served to demonstrate to the Southern beauties that even under adverse circumstances the Yankees did not forget their early lessons in politeness and gratitude. Darkness dispersed visitors and brought quiet. We again rest on "mother earth," huddling together like pigs to present united resistance to the damp earth and chilly night air. The writer gazed upward into the "dim-lit vault" above him, and was busy with his thoughts. "Andersonville," they say. "No chance for exchange, because of Confederate refusal to recognize colored troops. I'm certain I wouldn't live in Andersonville a week. "Uncle Sam" not likely to yield the point on color. Desperate alternative, but I'll take my chances in attempting to escape." There's a gully through a brier-patch. New light: escape by way of burial. Plan matured; trusty comrade officers assist. Tin cup, muscles, will, calculating ingenuity, friendly suggestions, briers cut to be stuck in the earth concealing the writer and present uninviting appearance to pedestrians, and cautious work, were brought into requisition, and the grave-digging was completed. During the labor, the captive's thoughts dwelt with some misgivings upon the imperative orders of the major, issued the day before in the presence of the prisoners: "Shoot stragglers without warning. If you catch a man hiding, bayonet him without a word. No nonsense." Intended for intimidation, eh? Well, it's safer to consider it in earnest. He thought also of the immatured plan to disarm our guards; how they were to be set upon simultaneously; how information of three companies behind us deterred us, and how disappointed some were when better counsel discouraged the attempt to reverse the situation. But the "grave." Col. Shedd, Thirtieth Illinois, now tendered his assistance. Boughs and grass were gathered; the adventurer fitted in; satisfaction. "All right, cover up." First came grass and boughs, then — "Oh here, Lieutenant, here are some things you'll need." Col. Scott presented some maps (linen) of the country, rolled up in which was a small pocket-compass, presented by Col. Shedd. A canteen was also presented, and served as a substitute for a pillow. A hurried hand-shaking, a hasty good-bye, and the burial proceeded. Earth came down upon him, pressing heavier and heavier. Old grass concealed fresh earth, and, pursuant to programme, stalks of blackberry were cut, and planted in the "new-made grave," in the hope that they would appear uninviting to pedestrians and better conceal the concealment.

Daylight approaches. Now the morning gray streams in one little ray through the small aperture ingeniously constructed at the head of the concealment for air. "Lieutenant" (a voice from above), "here are some rations for you, at your head, just under the surface." "Oh thank you!" was the muffled response; "but don't stop up the hole." An hour slowly passed; another — seemed like three. The pressure from above seemed to increase more and more; a ton couldn't seem heavier. The right side and arm were now without feeling — paralyzed; whole body in pain; pressure terrible. The suffering body suggested a reconsideration; ruled "out of order" as Andersonville came in view. A death-like chill now seemed to penetrate the body of the buried captive, as if threatening to freeze the vitals. To move would be a luxury, but a motion of the "foundation" would certainly demolish or disturb the upper stories.

July 27. — Broad daylight. Distant view of sunlight. My acquaintance entirely cut. Are their motives actuated by prudence or fear? Wonder if every thing is all right? Is there any fresh earth visible? Do the briers stand up properly? Considerable risk, this. Wouldn't like to be the digger of my own grave. Foolish risk, perhaps. But what can I do now but lie perfectly still? Unusual commotion above. Footsteps hastily approach the "brierpatch." A voice, "All right, Lieutenant; lay low; goodbye." (Retreating footsteps.) Encouragement and consolation. The "forsaken" indistinctly heard, "Hurry up your breakfast!" (breakfast!) and "Fall in!" The line extended in close proximity to the "missing" captive. "Column, right face! forward — march!" and the column was in motion. How distinctly can be heard the regular tread. A sudden heavy pressure, another; twice stepped upon, but by captives or captors remains a mystery. A mounted Confederate rode at the rear of the column, and the sound of the horse's feet beating on the hardened path is distinctly heard by the hidden prisoner; nearer and nearer approaching, now alarmingly close, and a welcome passage by. The loose earth rattled down through the narrow window, and the danger passed. The road reached by the column. A halt. "All right," rang along the lines, and the column moved southward. Glorious relief. The forsaken had chatted freely with a Confederate officer the previous day, and entertained some fear that on that account he might be missed the more readily by the officer. The Confederate rear-guards now drew rations from a wagon on the road, thereby necessitating further patience. Rations drawn, guards and wagon pass on; time is precious. Voices; a grunt; a craunching; crumbs chasing each other down the air-hole. A modest hog calmly devours my hidden rations, and leisurely passes on. Voices still: children. It must be investigated. A slow pressure of the head upward; a giving of the covering; a falling of the loose earth and dust into ears and eyes and down the neck (agreeable sensations!), and through a little mound of sticks and boughs and briers and dirt peered two anxious eyes over the recent "bed-chamber." A huge hog; a negress, with two white children, evidently searching for relics of Yankee visitation, were the only living things visible. What a deserted appearance; yet loneliness was never before so coveted. Joy! a slight rain falls with refreshing welcome, and drives the curiosity-hunters from the field. Is there a possibility that the ground is still watched? A listening; a further elevating of the miscellaneous mound. Sounds of horses feet; three cavalrymen pass on the adjoining road in the direction of the departed captives. A hasty lowering of the head; another reconnoissance. Raining copiously, and the water trickles through the covering and renders the "grave" untenable. Now! and with a bound and a spring the slimy, narrow concealment was cleared, and the adjoining timber entered at "double quick." What! another blue uniform? and gliding away through the timber like a deer. The captive stood spell-bound. The tall object finally turned, stopped, and looked as if surprised. A slow approach, an explanation, congratulations, uniting of destinies for present purposes. "What is your name, Lieutenant?" asked the companion. "Bailey, of Gen. M. L. Smith's staff; and yours?" "Lybyer," said he, "of the Indiana cavalry." Mutual expressions of satisfaction; "misery loves company" demonstrated. "You are very tall, Lybyer, but you appear very young for a soldier," suggested the officer. "I'm six feet and over, and seventeen years of age," said he. "Why, eighteen is the youngest enlistment in our army. How did you get in?" asked the officer. "Well," said he, "I got in on my length, I suppose." A united, hearty laugh.

It was not until after the writer reached the Federal lines that he learned that the prisoners were halted and counted when about half a mile from camp, and one officer reported as missing; that a patrol was immediately sent back, and, shortly after, shooting was heard, which all supposed was occasioned by the discovery of the concealed captive. Hence, when the special exchange between Sherman and Hood was effected, the fellow-captives reported the writer as undoubtedly killed. Doubtless the shooting was intended to produce that impression among the prisoners.

The floodgates of the skies seemed opened, and the rain fell in torrents. A retreat to the heart of the woods. The whole surface was inundated. We stood upon the elevated localities under the great trees, and mutely considered the situation, while the storm raged fearfully. We were as wet as water could make us; still, it was considered better to be out of the water than in it. Homeless, houseless, friendless, wet, cold, — such circumstances were well calculated to dampen the ardor and cool the zeal of the most ambitious, and to destroy the ecstacy which attended the first realization of freedom. For hours we silently stood, each in his own way contemplating the situation. The storm of wind and water raged fearfully, causing the woods to roar like old ocean. The aged oaks groaned dismally, and bowed their venerable heads to the gale. Toward evening the storm abated. Broken trees and swollen streams were left to attest its fury. "How did you get away?" asked the officer. "I was asleep in a brush-pile. I didn't wake up until after they'd gone; then I thought I'd go the other way," said Lybyer. "How did you get away?" "Buried myself," said the officer, with an explanation of the mode. We feasted on blackberries; water — liquid mud. Hungry. Twilight; we approach the road. A mansion; negro cabins in rear. Objectives — the blacks. A whispered consultation; we are unanimous in our opinion that the blacks are our friends. We reach the road. Hark! hoofs pattering on the well-washed road; approaching. We immediately drop behind a large bush, and lie protected from the mud on the grassy border of the field. We now hear the clanking of sabres, and human voices. A squadron of cavalry pass, clearly visible in the twilight. We had no inclination to interfere with them; they pass without challenge.

Opportunity presenting, we cross the road, and circle around the mansion (to avoid the dogs we had heard bark during the day) to the cabin of a negro. Halt! listen! Voices within — negro voices. The writer selected a small pebble from the ground, and tossed it through the darkness toward the door. It struck against the door with a loud crack. The door was softly opened. A voice, "Who dar?" "It's friends, aunty," said the writer; "come to the fence." "Who is you?" said she. "Come out and see," was the response; "we'll not harm you." She hesitatingly approached the fence, and was informed in a whisper, "We are Yankees, aunty." "Is you, sah? [Peering at our uniforms closely.] De Lord bless you, sah! Hi, hi! — and hab you done got away from our folks?" "Yes," came the response, "and we are wet through, and very hungry. Can you help us?" "I jess can; but dar's a white gal in dar now. When she's done gone, I'll call you," she said. We trusted her, and our confidence was not misplaced. We waited half an hour, when we were electrified by the announcement, "She's done gone, and I'se got some supper for you." We entered the humble hut, and there was spread for us her offering to the cause we represented. Wheat biscuits — glorious! warm corn-bread — luxurious! fried apples — excellent! raw apples — golden! Nothing prevented our enjoyment to the utmost of our capacities, which seemed almost unlimited, save an occasional remonstrance by our teeth, which had become somewhat sensitive after our free indulgence in blackberries. Lybyer had retained his haversack, and the writer had none. "Take dis yere one," said our benefactress, presenting a worn and greasy Confederate haversack. "Oh thank — thank you, aunty," replied he, grasping the coveted "grub-bag" eagerly. Near midnight; a glorious fire on the humble hearth; clothes drying nicely; boots drying on the feet — if taken off, no assurance of ability to replace them. We grow cheerful under the "limbering-up" process. Inquiries: "About thirty miles from Atlanta." First Yankees ever seen; would find negroes all friendly; if caught, might be killed. Rebs, "grand rascals;" — "no 'pendence on 'em." Our implicit confidence in the negroes became a settled fact. We counted on their indispensable assistance at the beginning; failing to obtain it, we knew the effort to reach our lines would prove futile. Consultation of maps and compass; filling of haversacks; expressions of gratitude; farewell; "De Lord bless you-uns;" departure.

Our plan was formed to adhere to a north-easterly course, avoiding, or at least independently of, roads and settlements, and reach the Northern Georgia Railroad, which extended from Atlanta to Augusta, near Lithonia or Covington, over thirty miles distant, and attempt to follow the iron conductor, as closely as circumstances would permit, westward toward Atlanta. To approach Atlanta directly would be a foolish attempt to pass through the lines of both armies; our aim was to pass around the Confederate right flank and into the Federal left, in which attempt we anticipated the necessity only of avoiding detached bodies of rebels, foragers, stragglers, or scouts, which generally select the flanks of their respective armies for their operations and observation, and where we considered the chances about equal in opportunities to conceal ourselves from Confederates and to disclose to Federals. North-eastward. Mud! mud! mud! The rain had rendered the ploughed fields almost impassable. Boots, which had seemed to defy efforts to pull off, now seemed to test our ability to keep on or to *pull out*. But roads *must* be avoided; the direction *must* be maintained; the north-star *must* be to the left of our front continuously; each step must place us one step further north. But all the fields were not ploughed, and relief was frequently afforded by reaching alternately pasture and woodland. At intervals we forded refreshing streams of water, gratefully exchanging the surplus weight of mud for that of water. So we marched, trudged, stumbled, occasionally tearing our way through clinging, affectionate brier-patches; but we were buoyant with hope, and strong with the first impulses of freedom. The woods possessed an impenetrable darkness, and all nature seemed at rest. The solemnity was broken only by the "voices of the night," and the occasional baying of distant watch-dogs. How did we maintain our direction while in the woods? Why, we had a pilot — a pilot that was bribe-proof, obeying only nature and nature's God — the little compass. How did we see the needle in the dark? The same nature that influenced the needle provided a light which illumined its surroundings within the compass. How? By sending it through the night air, inviting us to accept it. In what shape? In the shape of harmless little fire-flies —"lightning-bugs." Each successive captive fly crawling over the glass of the little military compass rendered the valuable services required of him, and was released from duty, unharmed, after the capture of his successor. Shining mercies; valuable allies; light to our gloomy pathway; friendship enkindled to endure through life: no injury shall befall any of your kind through me; no harm shall be threatened without my interposing plea in your behalf. We reach a grand old oak near the centre of a pasture, and wellnigh exhausted we cast ourselves upon the damp grass and stretched our weary frames.

A brilliant conundrum here provoked some discussion, in spite of surroundings: "Why are we like the compass?" repeated the writer. "I can't imagine. Let's see; is it because we are made up of brass and point?" "No, no," was the reply; "'cause we're pointing north." Dead silence. Lybyer smiled the smile of original genius. "But the needle points, not the compass," suggested the writer. "Well," ain't the needle part of the compass?" asked the other. "Yes," was the reply; "still, it's only the needle that points. Then we're only like a part of the compass, eh?" "The most important part," he rejoined. "Then your conundrum is not well put," said the writer, exultingly. "Well," said he, "say needle for compass." "Still you would be lame," replied the writer; "for we are not pointing north, but directly north-east." A united laugh. Slumber touched our weary eyelids, and we slept. An hour passed; we awoke. That sleep! Appreciation of the sufferings of Rip Van Winkle after his twenty-years slumber. Rheumatics — refractory joints — disobedient muscles — death-like chill — invitation to despondency — terrible pains. Onward march; fields, woods, mud, streams passed, and warmth returns to our chilled bones. The morning light is breaking, and the record of —

July 28th opens. The frequent crowing of cocks in various directions indicates a village or settlement. We reach the border of large, swampy woods; determination to "anchor" there for the day. We climb over a high fence, press through the marsh, and seeking a dry elevation, establish headquarters for the day, happy in the contemplation of gorging ourselves with the luscious watermelon which the writer had stumbled against *en route*, and had clung tenaciously to for miles of the weary night's march. What's that? Hounds, as we're alive! yelping and howling upon our pathway across the adjoining fields. Nearer and nearer. From elevated positions on stumps and saplings we observe the howling brutes following our path. Now they are at the fence, and where we climbed over. No followers; must be endeavoring to create an excitement on their own responsibility. Now their distressing howls penetrate through the forest, reëchoing like a dismal wail. Headquarters no longer considered tenable; hasty leave; rapid transit; swamp; water knee-deep; a stream. Glorious!

Down it we go, waist-deep in its shielding waters, about three-quarters of a mile. Dry land again. "That's the only way to hide scent from those bloody brutes, Lybyer," said the writer, almost breathlessly, and still clinging like grim death to the prized watermelon. "Listen!" The brutes have passed the fence, and are howling on our path through the timber. Now a dismal chorus of unearthly howls resounds through the woods. "They must have struck headquarters," said Lybyer, breathing heavily. On they rush, howling and bellowing, to the stream, whose protecting waters had conveyed all traces of the timid adventurers beyond the reach of the keen noses of the brutes. Up stream, and down stream, and across stream, howling and wailing, while two weary and drenched mortals stood with trembling anxiety awaiting the test of the experiment. The sounds became more infrequent and lighter; they ceased. Friendly stream! without thee, and a knowledge of thy virtue, how might the happy result be changed. "Those dogs have been used to huntin' niggers, I'll bet," said Lybyer, breathing freer, and bunglingly attempting to wring the lower parts of his pants. "They seemed savage enough to eat us, without regard to color," replied the writer. "Darn lucky escape," added Lybyer.

We discover another "island;" reëstablish "headquarters;" listen long and attentively; settle down for the day. Slight fall of rain. A disrobement, and double strength applied to twisting our wardrobes. "Twist for me and I'll twist for you." Rain ceases. Glorious sunlight streams through the thick foliage, with golden lustre, and myriads of lingering crystal drops sparkle and flash like diamonds in the tree-tops. Beautiful! Higher arose our genial friend "Old Sol," and two half-clad and tired refugees gladly basked in the warm rays.

"Breakfast," called the writer. "Come, Lybyer, we're going to cut a watermelon." A rusty knife brought into requisition; a struggle; a victory. The watermelon opened; invited a feast (?). "I don't believe that's a watermelon," said Lybyer, rather facetiously, gazing at the two parts of the prize. "What? Maybe you never saw this kind before," replied the writer, suddenly realizing that Lybyer was right, yet unwilling to acknowledge it abruptly. (I never was so taken in in my life, thought he silently.) "Kind?" said Lybyer, "That's the kind we used to call *gourds* in Indiana." The "secret" was out. "Why don't you eat it, Lieutenant?" inquired L., with a merry twinkle in his eye. "Have a piece?" asked the writer, evasively, passing half to L. "No, thank you," said he; "don't eat melons, 'cept for dessert." "The main objection to this melon is, it's green," said the writer, feigning disappointment. "Them kind 's always green," chimed in L. "All watermelons are always green, you know," said the writer. "All of 'em?" inquired L. "How about the ripe ones, then?"

"Ripe, yet always green—on the outside," said the writer, looking merrily full into L.'s face for a recognition of brilliancy. "Oh yaas, that way," said he, unappreciatively. "Now, this thing is green *inside* as well as outside — unfit to eat," and the two halves were tossed to one side contemptuously by the writer. It is often the case with woman's love, but the man's in this instance had "clung like ivy to a worthless thing." More sunlight enabled both to enjoy the sunny side of the joke.

More stripping, and wringing, and hanging to dry. That's all right; we were born this way; but still, don't want to be caught this way. Dry and don is the rule. Each sleeps and watches alternately; draw cuts for first sleep; each sleeps, each watches three hours; writer's watch common property; two heads decidedly better than one. Writer's turn to watch; L. snores like the "seven sleepers," — make it eight. Sounds of breaking limbs in the distance; two piercing eyes peering at us from the foliage; hog approaches; quite neighborly; grunts; curious; nearer. Ah, the "watermelon." Quite welcome, sir. Craunching and grunting; history of "watermelon," as a whole or in halves, ended; treated also to crackercrumbs; encourage company;" visitor all right; won't tell tales. Hum "Rock of Ages." Hogs like "music;" enchanted; motionless as a statue; a grunt; queer brutes; strong prejudices; headstrong; anti-German; Jewishly inclined; pork — ham — bacon — lard — pigs' feet — sausage — head-cheese. Three porker companions reënforce the first discoverer; all seem fond of hymns. Any relief from the dull drag of the weary hours acceptable. Dogs barking; cocks crowing. Must be near somebody's plantation.

Hark! Yes; a low, rumbling sound in the distance. Cannon! Continued distant sullen rumbling. That sounds business-like. [It was Hood's sallying attack on the old Army of the Tennessee, which changed position from the extreme left to the extreme right of the Federal lines. Result, six hundred and forty-two left dead on the field before incompleted entrenchments in process of construction, and a speedy and bloody repulse. It was Hood's last mad, vain attempt to raise the siege of Atlanta, and to free himself from the tightening grasp of Sherman's veteran army. Thousands of his best infantry were lost in the persistent attempt to escape the inevitable.]

Listen to that harmony of human voices in the other direction, — the plaintive songs of negro field-hands returning from work. How melodious, yet how mournful! How in keeping with the present delicious calm! What strange contrast with the sweet notes of nature's warblers, as they sport among the tree-tops, enjoying the last rays of the setting sun! A glimpse of the western horizon. Unparalleled beauty; marvellous brilliancy! The heavens aglow with golden light; crimson and purple and gold exquisitely and inexplicably blended; silvery-lined clouds floating in happy relief against the blazing glory beyond them, and fiery rays streaming far upward into the heavens; fantastic forms of cloudy images sporting before the enchanting beauty as if in ecstasy, bathing in the golden flood of evening's sunlight. "Lybyer," said the writer, "just look at that sunset; did you ever see the equal of that?" L. peeped through the foliage a moment, and turning away, muttered, "Have just as pretty ones in Indiana." "Maybe they've got another sun there," said the writer, perhaps a little sharply. L. remained silent.

Preparation for the march; dry as a chip; eager; we must make tracks lively to-night; time is precious. Hark! a voice, " Whoa, Dolly! whoa, Dolly!" Not for us. Carefully creeping toward the fence, and peeping through the shrubbery, the writer beheld, only a few yards distant, an individual endeavoring to catch his mare; slouch hat—coatless—long hair—thin, sharp features—Roman nose—goat beard—veritable Southern type—no questions—no acquaintance desired. Man mounts animal and departs. Almost ready; comfortable; happy in the anticipation of rapid strides homeward. Distant rumbling: cannon or thunder? Lightning, thunder—nearer, heavier—terrible crashes; lightning vivid, blinding; preliminary breezes, preceding great drops. Crushed hopes; blighted prospects; Egyptian darkness; floodgates open; torrents, torrents, torrents; summarily drenched to the skin; ardor cooled: sunlight of hope, storm of despair. No use waiting; all right. North-eastwardly through the descending torrents; mud, slippery; fields, pastures; stumbling through dark, wet woods; compass; fire-flies; direction. Awful dark; can't keep together; novel expedient; take hold of my coat-tail; better. Stumbling over logs and stumps; tearing through briers; butting against saplings; feeling along. Two hours passed; so has the storm, so are the woods. Open field; good time; rapid walking. By all that's holy, what's that? Suddenly heavy, unearthly sounds fill the air. We stand as if petrified; hearts in throat. A large drove of hogs suddenly aroused, "Hoff! hoff! hoff!" and a great rushing and running, creating noise sufficient to be heard across the field. What a fright; so unexpected. We knelt where we were, awaiting the possible result of the unseasonable uproar. No alarm; march resumed. Midnight. Indistinct outlines of large tree in centre of a pasture invite us to rest beneath its branches. We accept. Clothes wet; ground wet; every thing wet. But we are too tired to proceed further; we droop at the foot of the friendly oak, and are soon both fast asleep. Haversacks for pillows; a cold, cold sleep. Awakening; terrible sensation; joints glued together; desperate struggles; determined efforts; pluck. On our feet again. Victory! No warmth. We limp north-eastwardly; walk; warmer; good time. Reach a thick forest; feel along its border for road, path, or opening. None; *tempus fugit;* penetrate the gloomy woods; black; imagination feels the darkness; stumbling — down, up; down, up. It's disagreeable and painful to fall, but it's comforting to be able to rise after each fall. Bushes, undergrowth, logs, stumps, briers, trees wet. Their presence proved only by contact; eyes as useless as spectacles to a mole. Limb-snapped faces, sore shins, torn faces and hands, disordered clothing. Rather monotonous taking the lead, "bearing the brunt;" necessity, however. Lybyer's cavalry jacket is tailless; lucky fellow; way broken for him; but a frequent "ouch!" indicates that he too has stubbed a toe, snapped an eye, struck a shin, or caught a brier. "Direction?" a halt for observations; listen! No earthly sound save the voices of the night and our own whisperings. Where's our guide (fire-fly)? Abandoned us; the deserter. "A pretty fix;" heart of Georgia forest; stars obscured; very dark; danger of making exit where we entered, to realize we have endured and spent our failing strength to no purpose. Delightful surroundings; pleasant prospects; a consultation; a rest.

Look behind. The heavens are lit up with a lurid glare. A fire! another! another! Three fires; miles distant; our cavalry at work. Proposition to turn back voted down. Must be our boys; but where would they be when we could reach the fires? Fires miles apart, indicate a circling around toward the Confederate right flank; but will they continue to circle? or will they be driven or turn back, or go still further south? Our boys, sure, among the rebel wagon-trains, depots, mills, and railroads. No sound of conflict or skirmish. No "blue-coats" warming themselves at those fires now. Wish they'd come nearer. Brighter; red reflections cast upon the dark clouds away up in the heavens, lighting up the gloomy earth and sky like the fading colors of closing day; a bloody sky. Wish we were in the open — could see better. Can almost see the needle of the compass. Alas! not quite. Backs to the fading lights. Onward! Partial but sufficient repetition of recent experiences in progress. The fires render use of eyes possible.

Hist! another fire in advance of us. Can it be pickets? Plan of approach. Halt! listen! On, step by step; no sounds — refugees sleeping around the embers of a fading camp-fire — on all fours. Peculiar fire; right on it — ought to hear snoring — silent as death. We arise. No pickets — no refugees — no sleepers — no danger — nothing but a decayed log and its scattered pieces innocently phosphorescing in its vain attempt to brighten the surrounding gloom. Substitute for firefly — application to compass. Needle pointing northward, as usual; but we are *not* pointing north-eastward, as usual. We were not "turned completely around;" but we were not travelling according to programme — that's sufficient. New pilot — phosphorus. Heavens brighten; woods less gloomy; trees seen indistinctly. Pilot not as accommodating as the former; far less ability. Brighter still — morning gray. Excellent time; rapid progress — break ahead; the contemptible forest cleared. Daybreak. Wonder how many miles we made last night through that aggravating net-work.

Glory, hallelujah! nothing but a rail fence separates us from a veritable watermelon-patch — remember the last "watermelon." A charge — a capture; investigation of interior of a fine one. O luscious product of the vine! Oh, yum-yum! Deplorable limited capacity. Talk about table etiquette, and indelicate sounds while eating soup. Just listen at Lybyer. (Expect L. is thinking same thing about me.) Really difficult to tell who's making the most of that indecent racket. Two countenances hidden — buried, and revelling in the luscious delights of stolen sweets. Another, and another. "Why is eatin' these like eatin' soup with a fork?" "Give it up; yum-yum!" said L. "Hard to get enough of it!" United laugh; fortune had allayed caution. The morning sun now shone beautifully on —

July 29. — Arms and "otherwise" full of watermelons. Cautious retreat; slow movements not caused by lameness entirely. Inviting blackberry-patch; "headquarters;" berries large and sweet; pearly rivulet. Almost paid to endure the perilous passage through the tangled wildwood by night, to reach such happiness as this in the morning; consolation. But do people go blackberrying in this country? Improbable; bushes too full of past-ripe berries; marshy spot this; more inviting localities, especially after rain. "Anchor," subject to further orders, for the day. Avenue of escape in case of danger? The rippling little stream beside us—we can crawl up or down unseen. But what if surprised now? Escape impossible. Crawl up stream? Why, we can't bend over. Run? Why, we can hardly walk. We couldn't even surrender gracefully. Two old women armed with blackberry-baskets could readily take us. We couldn't even "explain"—"too full for utterance." "Dinner"— Soup: *L'eau de terre (a la ripple)*. Baked: *Pain de blé (a la mush)*. Entrée: *Melon d'eau, red.* Dessert: Confederate berries *(à l'Africaine)*. Ample for a king under like circumstances. Composed; stripping; wringing, drying process. Alternate "picket-duty." Taking observations of day sounds; plantation-houses out of sight, but within hearing. Bread rations gone; determination to "draw" a further supply, or fail in the attempt.

Evening. Rumbling of numerous wagon-wheels near by; must be a road; the "mansion" must be on that road, and the humble huts of sable friends must be in rear of the mansion. What road is that? Maps, compass consulted. It must be the main road leading east and west from McDonough. Are we east or west of that to-be-avoided town? That's the question; unsolved. Twilight; preparation; departure in single file. The well-worn road reached and crossed; cautious passage beside the road to approach and ascertain relative positions of high and low dwellings; object accomplished. The usual circuitous performance brought us to a fence which separated us only a few feet from the negro-cabins. Determined to trust to negroes again, and to make the second test of fidelity to the cause we represented. Listen! All quiet. A silent approach to a hut; scaling the fence that separated us; a peep through a friendly crevice; a negress and a white lady sitting silently, calmly gazing into the royal log-fire on the hearth. A large dog now came snuffing the air around the cabin, and observing the writer, barked furiously at him. A skip — a bound — a leap — fence cleared, and a double retreat to a neighboring peach-orchard — rest. Another approach to another cabin — end cabin; more cover for retreat. The writer cast a small pebble over the fence against the door. Crack! it sounded. No response; experiment repeated; great commotion within the cabin; shuffling of feet, and general bustle. Two or three negresses ran from the cabin's opposite door or window toward the "big house." Negro cautiously approached the fence. "Uncle, uncle," said the writer; "here, we're Yankees." "Uncle" shook like a leaf in the wind. "De Lord bless us," said he, "is de rest comin'?" "Hope so, uncle," said the writer. "Are you friendly?" "Lor' yes," said he; "we's all friendly, sho." The immediate importance of overtaking and quieting the timid negresses who had sped toward the "big house" was impressed, and fleet feet carried information which transformed fear into curiosity. The fugitives silently returned; the exciting news spread quickly from cabin to cabin; a group of sable admirers stood awe-stricken before real, live, veritable Yankees. First Yankees seen. "Such beau'ful uniforms!" "Such nice gemmen!" Too much commotion here; retreat to heart of peach-orchard suggested, and executed. Prime object, something to eat. Men followed us to our retreat; women remained in cabins to vie with each other in preparing and presenting elegant repasts. Glorious prospect. Peach-orchard retreat reached. Questions — explanations — congratulations — antics — admiration. Women approaching stealthily, one by one, bearing warm biscuits (elegant), sweet fried bacon (grand), hot corn-coffee, "'lasses sweet'nin'" *(coup-de-grace)*. Did ever such fortune overtake such forlorn creatures before? Their enlarged ideas concerning the Yankee and his capacity found illustration in the amount of these offerings. They seemed to provide enough to feed a full company of infantry. We crammed and stuffed; full. Questions curious, absurd, and ridiculous; ideas right on the main question — woefully contorted on some of the incidentals. The war, slavery, freedom, Lincoln, Grant, Sherman — almost everything and everybody.

News. One of our friends who has been in the "big house" returns almost breathless, and imparts the information that the Yankees have burned Lovejoy's Station on the Atlanta and Macon Railroad, twenty miles south of Atlanta, and were momentarily expected on the road we had just left, *en route* to the Federal left flank. Glorious news; beaming countenances; congratulations; dancing for joy! "When was the station burned?" "Last night," the messenger replied. "We saw the fires," chimed in L. "What command — did you hear?" asked the writer. "Command of Mr. Sherman, I reckon," replied the messenger, not comprehending my meaning. "I mean, who was the head one of our boys at Lovejoy's?" repeated the writer, simplifying. "Oh, dat," said he; "why I heerd de white folks talkin' 'bout Mr. Kilpatrick's *calvary* comp'ny. Oh, dey's comin' sho; I can a'most feel 'em now." Maps, compass; great excitement. Negro cabins deserted, may attract attention of white folks. "No, no, — hi, hi! — dey's too sceered." Caution cautioned; plan of action; the road to be watched all night. "George" is to take us in charge and guide us to safe cover within one hundred yards of the road. Haversacks overstuffed with the remains of our royal repast; comforting quilts furnished in abundance by friendly hands. Negroes not "on duty" to return to respective cabins and remain quietly; secrecy and safety. We arose to execute the plan; surrounded by dusky friends, who handle and investigate clothing, caps, boots, complimenting every thing, of course, in the highest terms. Rather diffident in the company stood a modest creature, whom the writer now recognized as the "white lady" he had seen while peeping through the cabin's logs; question; confirmation; poorly clad, but very beautiful; white, yet accounted "black;" worse still, a slave. Conversation; manifestly much pleased at my preference and attention; "house-girl;" intellectually towering high above her crude companions; fine features — Grecian — no African trace; fair, rounded face; large, lustrous, brown eyes; form, so far as can be judged through rags, a model for the sculptor. How natural the conclusion: blood of the master reduced to slavery. If we could only stop here; if slavery were all; if absolute dominion were out of consideration. To the slave, beauty is a blighting curse. The richer the gifts of nature, the swifter and surer the demolition of chastity by beastly "proprietors." Owned — "bought with a price" — fiendish traffic in one's own flesh and blood; repulsive thoughts. "Civilization." "How long? How long?" The question is being answered daily by the distant rumbling of Federal cannon, and nightly by the lurid glare that paints the Southern sky. We also here again listen to the "stories" told the blacks by the whites concerning the horrid mental and physical natures of the Yankees. Many of them are too ridiculous even to repeat, and all of them disclose desperate efforts to conceal the truth by vainly attempting to strengthen the superstitions of the ignorant. Rational explanations. Reception and supper decidedly warm. Grateful "good-night" to our variously colored friends. "George." "Headquarters" for night; midnight retirement; quilts great luxuries; glorious slumber in the woods. Daybreak, sunlight; still we slumber.

July 30. — Quite early this morning we were regaled by the sounds of heavy cannonading Atlantaward. Never appeared so close nor so distinct as now, since taking our leave of that doomed city. The sounds of the great guns roll heavily through the morning air, creating quite a martial spirit at " these headquarters." [It was the Federal batteries shelling the stronghold.] A stream of clear water — must be the same upon which we "encamped" yesterday in the distant blackberry-patch. Luscious wash. Breakfast, as is one, from our haversacks. Where's George? Strange absence; faith, hope. Take extra precaution; prepare for emergencies.

we shift "headquarters" to another position, commanding view of the former; also concealing ourselves from view of any venturer upon the well-beaten path extending near by our retreat. First night of rest since capture; animal spirits returned; even disposed to be frisky; strong as a regiment. Noon; no tidings — no appearance; conjectures — misgivings — late afternoon. Writer left L. on guard, and cautiously proceeded to the stream near by, for water and wash. At the stream—unconsciously too near a path. Commotion and shouting. The writer quickly looked up in the direction whence came the sounds, and saw a cow coming rapidly down the path on a run; a dog was descried following the cow, and two white boys were following the dog. To fall back toward headquarters would result in almost certain exposure — no time to think — immediate action. "Sic her! sic her!" shouted the boys. The writer ran into the thickest part of the woods; the cow saw him, and left the path to follow so good an example — persistent follower; race long and exciting; curving around tree-clusters — darting through thickets—Yankee — cow — dog — boys — a fence; glorious partition — at it, over it in a twinkle; corn-field retreat—awaiting developments. Gratified that the mandate "Sic her," still continued unchanged to "Sic him." The dog forced the cow from the fence, and the race continued, minus the "leading" character. The contrary brute turned homeward, and soon the sounds of the chase ceased. Fool cow—sagacious dog—astute (?) boys—protecting fence—fortunate escape—hasty return to headquarters — half mile. L. all right. Tale of adventure; lucky — laughter — tired.

Evening. Through the thick foliage, stepping cautiously, half crouching, we descry a human form approaching our former quarters. Lying flat upon the ground, we silently watch the stealthy movements; black face — confidence. He looked at the marked tree, and then at our recent bivouac, and seemed nonplussed. He peered mysteriously in various directions; we arose — he discovered and approached us — it's George; "brought little lunch" — thoughtful George. "Thanks." Living high now. "What's the news?" Explanation—the Federals had not arrived, but some of the rebels had, and stopped at the "big house" — colored folks crestfallen. Recuperated — refreshed — restless — determined.

Late evening. Peach-orchard; supper No. 2; repetition of first, with warm, veritable apple-pie added. (Ye epicures.) A feast; profuse expressions of gratitude; filling of haversacks; many a "God bless you;" a hearty farewell, and under the guidance of George we were conducted to the main Decatur road extending northward to Decatur, six miles west of Atlanta. "Little travelled; safe to proceed cautiously on this road." Whispered gratitude — silent hand-shaking; George returns. We proceed on the road cautiously northward, rapidly, silently, single file. Plan of procedure: The writer constituted the "advance guard;" L. comprised the "rear guard." Any approach to either end of the "column" was to be communicated to the other by the casting of a pebble, in which case the alarming end was to unite with the other for consultation; distance between "detachments," forty feet. This method considered best. Two make more noise than one; no unnecessary talking — hear better.

Lybyer deserves more particular mention—necessary to assist reader in fully comprehending situation. He was very tall, disproportionate — not agile, sluggish — mild-mannered — honest — dull — inexperienced — indiscreet at times, careless — full appetite — enjoys sleep — sometimes morose — lacks nerve — tractable — stumbles — steps on dry limbs, kicks rocks, noisy getting over fences; apologizes — "can't help it;" does his best, not to blame; excited in presence of danger — good-natured — carries a leathern "valise" on each foot — makes his companion nervous and doubting, especially when silence is the great *desideratum* — companionable, welcome, agreeable, trustworthy—desirable, except in the presence of danger, when solicitude extends to foes and friend alike — rather prone to — But we all have our faults and weaknesses, and by casting a glance within, can find sufficient food for contemplation, relieving of the assumed necessity of dwelling upon the failings of others, even though the failings be presented interwoven among recognitions of worth.

Still northward — rapid marching — several miles gained — a little fatigued. Small, abrupt rise in the road; abrupt fall immediately beyond it. Sufficiently advanced to obtain a view of Walnut Creek bottom — a fire by the roadside. Warning pebble apprizes L. of danger. Halt! Observation — gurgling waters of the creek — brighter blazing of the fire — Federals, refugees, or rebels? L. placed in concealed position beside the road, while writer attempts a reconnoissance off the road; cautious approach — wagons — stacked arms — sentry in road, lazily pacing to and fro — company sitting around fire, chatting — dialect decidedly Southern — sentry approaches fire — shining rifle-barrel, glistening buttons, *gray* uniform. That's sufficient. A silent return to L.; disclosure of the information, "They're rebs!" Departure, with intent to circle around a difficulty which we would not attempt to remove. Crossing fields, we reach in safety the creek several yards below the fire — quite a creek — dashing waters — friendly sounds — noise of stream favorable for our purpose. A slight elevation; screen of foliage; quiet observation — wagon-guards. Too near the creek; log crossing; up and down the stream to find safe crossing; none — too deep to ford, too swift to swim. Whispering consultation; the log crossing our only present hope. "What!" said L., "over that log?" "It's a risk, but what else can we do?" asked the writer. "We can't stay here long thinking about it, either." Desperate plan — fortunate miniature roar of the current. "We'll have to go right by 'em," said L., recalling the fact of danger. "Well, the stream's racket will help us," said the writer; "and we must get over as soon as we possibly can, consistent with safety." Perfection of plan; writer ahead, L. following some fifteen feet behind — on all-fours — cautious — slow progress. Halt! listen! On! Fire blazes up — light shining now full in our faces — end of the coveted log in view; underbrush foliage only separates it a few feet from the group around the fire; fire blazes still brighter. (Really believe I'd get out of this if I could; as much danger to "back" now, as to go ahead.) Log didn't seem so uncomfortably near before we approached — bushes didn't seem half so small from distance. We crawl to protecting shadow of small bush, and lie and listen. Lybyer doing exceedingly well; moves with me, and halts with me. Only an occasional slight cracking of limbs and twigs, but harmless in the noise of rushing waters. End of log almost within reach, yet how many "miles" away! Reconsideration; great risk — ugly customers — thoughts of cold, damp slumbers on the open ground; determination — snail-like progress — end of log reached. Listen! Above the sounds of the noisy stream, the writer heard the voice of one of the guards relating a story to his companions seated around the camp-fire. Separated from recapture now, only by a few feet and the shielding foliage of a clump of bushes, through which streamed the lurid light of the fire. The story — a *woman* in the case, as usual — hope it's a long story, and interesting. There's that sentry nearing the group, evidently to get the point of the tale — glistening rifle-barrel. Wonder how Lybyer's making it? Won't wait to hear the upshot of the story — trust the others have more interest in it. Rebs rolled in blankets, sleeping near fire — army wagons — foragers — wagon-guards — hardly *ten feet* distant; could almost reach that officer's hat! Over! over! "Suppose I should be overtaken or met on this ominous log?" Over the centre of the splashing waters, and while waiting to witness L.'s performance, silently filled canteen from the stream below. L. moves like a snake upon the log, and, in a manner admirable, progresses northward, reaching the writer. No longer snail-paces; we arise and foot it rapidly to the other shore—safe! well done; whispering mutual admiration and congratulations. More caution.

But enemies and danger suddenly sprang from an unexpected source. The horses which were tied to the wagons had taken the alarm, and exhibited decided evidences of great uneasiness; pawing the ground and snorting loudly — pricked ears toward our side of the stream. A glance at the group convinced us that their attention had been attracted to the conduct of the animals, and was now directed across the creek! No time to waste — action — steep rise before us — thick growth of underbrush—up we glide, as rapidly as safety permitted; brisk walk — half-way up — sudden cracking and snapping. Alas! L. had selected a route of his own, and was entangled, apparently hopelessly, in a brush-heap; the struggle continued unabated — L. manifestly desperate! The listening Confederates now sprang to their feet, some seizing their rifles — demolishing the regulation stack of arms which had graced the picture, glistening in the reddened glow of the fire, and bearing satisfactory evidence of military training. The sentry in the road, in a half-whispering voice, hurriedly uttered something to his aroused companions, and came to the water's edge. Now they all seem to stand with ears, eyes, and mouths wide open, gazing up on the hillside, apparently wondering what could mean the occasional cracking sounds still continuing. Two now stand at the end of the log, holding above their heads large burning brands which cast a flood of light upon the hillside — villainous persistency — darkness turned to day — to move would certainly betray our positions and invite a rifle-shot. Now'll come a challenge; it will be ruin to respond, it may be death to refuse to respond — no pathway out of this scrape visible. Respond, "A friend;" 'twill cause momentary hesitation, at least; then run the other way, and take the remaining chances— will act on that suggestion — tormenting glare — light as day — very awkward extremity; one arm drawn carefully and slowly upward in the attempt to conceal the face, the other twisted in the attempt to interpose it between glaring Confederate eyeballs and a suggestive row of glittering Federal coat-buttons — motionless as the neighboring oak; daring to watch opposite movements with but one eye, and that partially concealed behind elbow wrinkles of blue cloth; subdued sounds from the brush-heap, but no challenge. What can that mean? Those fellows can't be regular soldiers — so much the worse for us, if caught. Here comes a fellow with a fresh brand blazing over his head — he is crossing the log, brand in one hand, rifle in the other; another approaches the log, rifle in hand — sentry standing in road, "arms, port." Still no challenge, no shot — "green troops;" time for action here. A loud whisper: "Lybyer, save yourself" — an abrupt turn, a leap, and the writer bounded up the hillside, joyfully disappointed at not realizing the dreaded expectation of a shot and a whizzing bullet. A sudden additional cracking of dry limbs, and L. was also free, and making excellent time up the hillside. We united on the level field above, and without following the terrible example of "Lot's wife," ran as fast as frightened, hopeful fugitives could run, — not directly northward, and away from the recent scenes, — not in the direction which would naturally invite pursuit, — but circled around, even to the extent of reaching the bank of Walnut Creek again, less than a mile below. A rest; almost breathless; water; narrow escape. "Thought we were gone, one time," said L.; "when that fellow came over with his torch." Congratulations—warnings—compass—fire-flies—direction—forward—steady marching, without interruption, until overtaken by the morning gray of—

July 31. — Scan surroundings for favorable spot to reestablish "headquarters." We never select such spot with a view to comfort, or because beautiful, or elevated, or dry—*safety* is the prime consideration, before which all others must yield. Large brier-patch selected—small stream gushing through it; we trample down the thick vines, and appropriate a few square yards for our purpose—no deed, no license; trespassers (don't deny it)—blackberries in luscious, tempting clusters. Stealing? Deny it; foraging—at most, confiscation. Breakfast from our full haversacks (bringing kind remembrances of our variously colored friends on the other side of romantic Walnut Creek) and blackberries. Where can we be? Maps, compass—conjectures. Not a solitary domestic sound—must be distant from plantation or road—even our little feathered friends seem to have deserted us, and no longer peer at us from neighboring limbs with curious gaze, nor enliven us with their sweet songs. Abandoned—drowsy. For the first time, by day, we carelessly omitted to alternately watch and sleep, and both were soon sleeping soundly—tired out. When we awoke, after an hour's sleep, the sun was shining brightly, and its warm rays penetrating through the thin protection rendered our position uncomfortably warm — hot; retreat impossible. We find that some relief is afforded even by the scanty shade of the briers around us, through which we had torn to our present position in the heart of the patch; smallest service is acceptable. Thanks.

"The daisy, by the shadow that it casts,
   Protects the lingering dew-drop from the sun."

Tall, thorny "daisies" these — two innocent "lingering dew-drops" — elongated comparisons; alternately watching and sleeping remainder of the day. Dark, ominous clouds rolled heavily in the sky, bringing evening's welcome hour sooner than expected — early start to-night. Threatening clouds; how they roll and surge; now cramped in contact, now swelling out and rising like moving mountains — storm-tossed ocean above us. "Water in them clouds," said L., looking upward pensively. "Sublime," said the other. "See how they toss and swell; look at that monster mountain of cloud; perfect picture, with its snow-capped summit, lofty brow encircled by fleecy clouds; and see the raging billows beating impulsively against its base. What sublimity!" "I don't want to get wet," added L., evidently entertaining disagreeable recollections of the past, and a practical realization of the present. Vivid flashes of lightning. See how they disclose great cavities — how they lighten deep caverns; how they set forth, in bold relief, crags and peaks and promontories; now dancing and chasing each other among fantastically formed fleecy images, run fine, vivid, fiery sprites — now sporting lightly with sunny crowns, that garnish dignity — now angrily flashing with a sudden glare among cloudy mountain rocks, followed by deep, crashing tones of "heaven's artillery;" the earth trembles; the deep-toned thunder rolls and reverberates through the heavens, ending in faint rumblings in the distant sky. "Grand!" exclaimed the writer. "Don't see any thing very grand in getting soaked through again," said L. "Wish we could strike shelter somewhere — another night's journey spoiled." Practical L. "Let's seek shelter," said the writer — maybe we can strike a cabin, or a barn, or a haycock, or something else, and keep dry." Agreed — departure — tearing through our surroundings, and reaching *terra firma*. No house, no cabins, no sheds, no shelter, save the trees; now "fumbling" for the lost main Decatur road — bearing in its supposed direction.

Hark! rumbling of wagon-wheels — numerous. We're very near a road; sounds approaching; still nearer; concealment — point is to see, and not be seen. Here they come, — one, two, three, — several wagons loaded with household furniture — refugees. Trouble in the air; fleeing from expected Yankees — splendid surface indications. Their distress our glory — they avoid what we seek; Yankees common objects of interest, but in opposite meaning. Another and another wagon-train — three trains, several wagons in each. Some commotion in affairs military must be the mainspring of their hurry and action — men (*a la* rear-guard) unarmed, on horseback. Great drops of rain; thicker; torrents — raging tempest; of course, summarily wet to the skin—standing under a huge oak for "protection." Writer looked at L. through the blinding rain — rim of his hat turned down, and the pearly waters flowing off in a circular cataract around his dejected countenance — that's the advantage of a hat — writer wears cap. A bid for some recognition, by peering inquiringly at the hardly discernible features beyond the miniature cascade — recognition — a roguish laugh for encouragement — response by L. by a silent, grim grin. Half-hour passes; storm subsides; all nature dripping wet.

We were not aware of our proximity to a path through the woods, leading to the neighboring road, and of course could not account for the clattering of hoofs over a stony portion of the path, and behind us. Sudden as a shock appeared, only a few feet from us, a horse, upon which was mounted a woman — too late to move — too late to speak. The writer stood with back against the old oak, perfectly motionless; L. suddenly sprang behind the same tree. The rider's attention was evidently attracted by the movement. She suddenly looked, and immediately her eyes met those of the writer — a surprised gaze on the one hand — a mild, assuring, harmless observation on the other. Passing, she turned her head and continued the same anxious, inquiring look until lost to sight amid the foliage. We listened — it was the lady excitingly urging her steed to greater effort. "Now what?" asked L. "She saw us, sure." "Why, out of this immediately." "She's only a woman," added L. "And, like most other women, she has gentlemen friends," quickly added the other, attempting an appropriate finish to the sentence. Thoughts of possible consequences; might not be agreeable to all concerned. Double-quick; clearing the timber — friendly blackberry-patch; briers, water, mud — concealed.

Sounds of more refugee wagons. Darkness without deception — frequent distant flashes in the heavens, from which came no reports, save an occasional sullen rumble. The retreating storm; darker — lightning flashes vividly; sharp and irregular; blinding — eyesight rendered worthless — brilliant electrical display — nature's pyrotechnics; rapid, almost constant alternate lighting up of earth and sky, and impenetrable darkness; two extremes — deep black curtain of nature, fitfully rising and falling alternately, exhibiting glaring revelations of indefinite and weird scenery. Frogs, and crickets, and whippoorwills unusually happy and correspondingly noisy — dreamy influences. Present *desideratum* — the main Decatur road; we rather abruptly left it to our left (westward) at Walnut Creek "skirmish," and it must still be to the west; hence temporary new direction, north-westward; compass, fire-fly — our course indicated and taken; less than half-hour's march, while feeling our way along amid the darkness, rendered darker by the sudden, fitful brilliancy, very damaging to eyesight, we reach a wide, hardened road, extending north and south. "That's it — no road between us and the main Decatur — must be it." Temptation to exchange chances in the wet and muddy fields for the hard road too great for resistance. Clothes wet through, heavy, muddy; misfortune enough without adding to it by struggling through miry fields and gloomy woodland, instead of making rapid time on the hard, well-washed road. Tormenting antics of electricity less brilliant — thanks. Give us inky darkness as a welcome change.

Northward, northward; rapid strides—no conversation; single file; excellent time; hope — midnight. Listen! "What can that be at this hour of night?" It's hammering or chopping — dim outlines of a house beside the road, on the rise of ground beyond the depression before us, from which the sounds proceed. Male voices distinctly audible — we cautiously approach to the little rippling stream which crosses the road through the depression — quenching thirst — filling the canteen afresh — discussing the situation in whispers. "Can it be possible that 'our boys' are in that house? possible that here is the Federal advance which caused the commotion among the fleeing refugees witnessed the evening before?" Possible, probable; yet caution — how easy to be mistaken; danger of over-confidence in circumstances and appearances. Voices of men still heard — hammering at intervals; would willingly give the only remaining valuable, my watch, to know the sentiments of those persons, or to see the color of their uniforms. Soldiers? Of course they're soldiers; no bodies of men travel these roads but soldiers; none other would be permitted, if they would travel them. The magic power of that great "tell-tale," the camp-fire, is absent; can't even discover but a very faint light in the house — probably the hearth-fire for cooking. Plan of operations: L. to perform the arc of a circle on the side opposite the house, leaving the fence here, circling around and reaching the fence again at a point corresponding to present position on the opposite side of the house; the other to proceed cautiously inside the fence to a point opposite the house, and endeavor to determine the meaning of the noises and the color of the uniforms of the inmates; the one to await the coming of the other at the designated spot. L. started out, and was soon lost in the darkness — the other stepped cautiously along the fence toward the object to be attained, and reached a point immediately across the road, opposite the house, and, as

subsequent developments will indicate, *silently* rested his
arms on the fence and listened, with eyes steadily fixed
on the building; no light now, no sound — silent as the
grave. Looks like a church, or anywhere North would
pass for a school-house. A sudden hawking, or clearing
of a throat, on the same side of the road as was the
listener, and within six feet (if the paralyzed senses could
judge of distance), drove the blood immediately to the
heart! The venturesome listener stood as if instantly
petrified — not a movement of a muscle, and breathless;
helpless, and lost in absorbing wonder! Dumbfounded
beyond description, his surprised eyes now witnessed the
careless knocking of a pipe against the stock of a
shouldered rifle, the falling sparks dimly revealing in the
darkness glittering buttons and *gray* uniform! Oh, for
one moment of magic power to silently sink into the
earth! Slowly returning senses. "How did I get here?"
How to get away; "wait, — I can do nothing but wait;"
waited nearly one mortal minute — seemed an hour; no
change in the terrible situation — movement of the dreaded
object — it's only to bring the butt of the rifle to the
ground, but it created a sensation in a quarter he least
suspected — indicates an intention to stay. Wonder if he
ever *sits on a fence?* Horrifying thought! Waiting perilous in the extreme — departing equally perilous; fearful
dilemma — one horn a bayonet, the other a bullet. Surrender? Never! Recapture inevitable? Not until the

very last chance, however imperceptibly thin, has been taken and fails.

Almost involuntarily the form of the adventurer slowly and silently sank toward the ground. The "very last chance" seemed to hang on the creaking of a boot or cracking of a joint. The ground was reached; a position slowly attained on "all-fours"—a silent and slow "heading" away from the fence; a breathless retreat; one hand, one knee—one at a time, feeling carefully with each before pressing, and silently removing or avoiding twigs or other suspicious substances; and thus, with gilded hope in every movement, and warning caution in every inch gained, the distance between the sentry and the fugitive was slowly and surely lengthened. More distance; more hope; less caution—forty feet away! The crawler arose silently and looked through the darkness toward the fence—an involuntary shudder—short distance—long trip; nearly an hour—nervous excitement too great—relapse; head pillowed in soiled hands—a slight fainting spell; only a moment.

"Where's Lybyer? No telling what he might think or do." Approaching the appointed meeting-place—halt; hark! whistling. "That must be L.—right direction;" cautious approach. If separated by day, the familiar whistle of "Bob White" was to indicate our whereabouts; if by night, the more difficult imitation of the whistle of the whippoorwill was to be attempted. Three o'clock in the morning; "Bob White" from neighboring fence — hasty approach. "Rebel pickets at that house!" excitement — unseemly haste dismounting from fence; down comes end of a rail with a racket. "Fell off itself" (of course it did) rails frequently become refractory; safety only in avoidance — ugly companions — not reliable. Rapid marching; single-file difficult — road again; excellent time — a fork in road; "which is which?" maps, compass, fire-flies, conjectures. While in consultation, we were aroused by approaching sounds in the road — queer sounds; horses or men? Tinkling of a canteen, indicating measured tread of its owner — probably the "relief guard" marching to the house on the road — maybe foragers, sensibly preferring to march during cool night rather than during hot day. We conclude not to permit these night marauders to "pass in review" before us; we have had excitement enough for present purposes, hence we move rapidly westward across the fields; then northward, penetrating and traversing thick, tangled woodland, and muddy fields. Shortly before daylight we happily entered woods of pine trees — no brush, no briers, no obstructions of any kind — rapid progress — pass small hut — dog howls dismally at us; brute continues howling long after we have passed the object of his faithful protection; must be a hound — other dogs *bark*.

Sudden bright red glare north-westwardly. (Atlanta!) Federals not driven back yet? Unaccountable quiet, however, considering that two great armies are confronting each other. Puzzling speculations — a temporary rest in the pines; we select concealed spot beneath protecting pine limbs, and stretch our weary bones on the cold, wet earth. No news; no encouraging sounds of cannon — ominous silence Atlantaward — doubts, fears, speculations, conjectures, ignorance — enemies in enemy's country — thoughts of home, of friends, of companions in arms, of chances of meeting them again, of glowing firesides, of beaming countenances, all in contrast with the present. Raining. How hath the poet painted our situation: —

"My life is cold and dark and dreary;
It rains, and the wind is never weary.
My thoughts still cling to the mouldering past;
But the hopes of youth fall thick in the blast,
And the days are dark and dreary."

Disconsolate. At last sleep came and touched the weary eyelids. The rain fell gently, dripping through the pine limbs upon the slumbering forms of those who lie dreaming of distant homes and warm firesides. We awoke, cold, wet, stiff, sore, and downhearted — very existence miserable. Surrender as prisoners? No; unanimously prefer to die in the woods rather than take the chances of living in a rebel prison. To escape the latter is what we have suffered and risked so much for, and we will continue to take our chances of life and of returning to our lines, in the woods, as cheerfully as possible accepting all the threatening consequences.

August 1. — Foggy — rations gone; we must seek assistance. We proceed through the lonely pines, making desperate efforts to get our limbs and joints in working order, yet never uttering a word. A yearning — not for food, not for drink, not for comforts, not for the Federal lines, not for warmth, not for friends, not for safety; a deeper yearning for a *something* which none of these wants could supply — a longing for some sympathy; some love, to partially fill the vacancy in the heart; a nearer relationship, a more satisfactory and closer communion with the spirit form which had seemed to hover near, encouraging by its smiles and presence through dark, discouraging hours, through all dangers and hardships and trials, through surrounding gloom. When shrouded by disappointment's mists, and when the spirit fainted under the burden of despair, then was the presence of this heavenly spirit manifested in the strengthening and lifting-up of the drooping soul. Yet there's a void in the heart like the void in the household, and the soul grows weary in indefinite contemplation: —

> "Weary, so weary of wishing
> For a form that has gone from my sight:
> For a voice that is hushed to me ever,
> For eyes that to me were so bright."

How do memory's nimble fingers speedily gather holy impressions and associations of childhood and of manhood, and arrange them in crowded clusters around the dearest of all earthly names. What name is brighter, purer, holier, than that of "mother"?

A brisk walk through the pines, of about an hour, brought us to oak timber; we reach a creek — quite a river; we cross on a log, and select a spot in the rather open woods for headquarters. Daylight; dangerous to proceed further — dangerous to stop; novel expedient; fortunate enough to retain pocket-knives, and with their aid branches are cut, and a very deceiving concealment improvised. Breakfast: corn-bread mush, "colored;" starvation sauce. Encouragement — domestic sounds; we can almost observe our requisitions for rations honored; strong faith; a short trip of observation; expectations realized, — plantation; plantation without negro cabins and occupants would be no plantation for us; a path through woods nearly quarter of a mile distant; we easily *command* it — with our eyes; seems freshly travelled. Repose; watching for sights, listening for sounds, alternately; at least one pair of eyes bearing constantly on the distant path through the open woods; at last vigilance was rewarded — negroes, apparently field-hands, passing; resolution to hail the first sole negro who passes; opportunity presented — rapid walking to head him off — approach — negro still whistling; nearer; still unattracted. "Heigh-ho! Sam!" He stopped as suddenly as if struck with a bullet! a silent, steady, astonished, inquiring gaze at the stranger in a blue uniform. "Come here, off the path, Sam," said the writer, patronizingly. "Sam" stood as motionless as an oak — a half-subdued inquiring gaze was the only response. "See here a minute," said the other, beginning to experience some misgivings about the African. Half smiling, half doubting, and with a hesitating step, he slowly approached. "Who is you, sah?" asked he, as if prescribing a condition precedent to further approach. (Trust; faith.) "I'm a Yankee," said the other, looking intently into the dusky countenance for an interpretation of possibly concealed feeling, which the illumination of the features might be calculated to hide. "Fur troo, sah? Lord bless my soul! Dey say de Yankees *do* dress in blue." "Yes, Sam," replied the other, assuringly. "Can't you tell by my speech?" "You don't talk like none o' our folks, dat's shoo. But I nebber seed a Yankee, and dunno." "Are you friendly to the Yankees, Sam?" inquired the writer. "I is, sah, fur fact — no mistake," he said quickly, with considerable emphasis. Genuine sentiment. "Well, I have a companion near by; and we are very, very hungry. Can you get us something to eat?" asked the other. "Wait a bit," said he. "I'll go and tell Cæsar, sly, and bring him to you." "Who's 'Cæsar?'" asked the other. "He's a mighty big friend o' you folks;" and off he started rapidly down the path after "Cæsar." Writer returned to L. — caution; watching; "Sam" returns with "Cæsar" — rude introduction; two pair of eyeballs entirely surrounded with white. "Don't live 'bout yere; belong to a refugee named Darby, who is camping near." Rations "scace," but willing to divide; unanimous consent to the proposition — very hungry. They depart; we take the usual precautions; they return; rations — corn bread, good! hot bean-soup, glorious! apples, fine! We take the "course" from top to bottom; sauce (superior to any furnished by the finest first-class hotels), hunger; gratitude — inquiries; maps — compass. Plantation near? "Yes, — Smith's." "Cæsar" in the *rôle* of "envoy extraordinary" to the "foreigners" of Smith's plantation — will return near evening; caution; departure; evening; return — mission well performed. "Smith's folks crazy to see you." Cæsar to act as pilot after dark; Cæsar and Dan (miscalled "Sam") advised to return to refugee teams, to allay any suspicion which might have been created by their absence, and remain there until after dark. The future and the horizon brighten together.

"Behind the clouds the sun is shining."

After-dark came, and so did faithful Cæsar; we were piloted to the road near Smith's plantation. Perhaps over-cautious, but refused to venture further until met and assured by one of Smith's negroes — the word carried — return, and with it came "Peyt," one of Smith's slaves. He seemed delighted to meet us. Peyt's complexion was as black as the night; he spoke in broken plantation idiom, but expressed himself accurately, and evidenced an extraordinary amount of uncommon sense — he proved a cheerful and valuable ally. In as good language and with as graceful manner as possible he informed us that a "big supper" awaited us at the cabin of his sister, "Aunt Mary." Accepted — trusty escorts — through an orchard — circling around to the cabin-door of "Aunt Mary." A peep in disclosed a room full of curious, excited negroes. "No, this will not do — too much commotion; too much risk." Plan: post trusty young negroes about fifty feet out on every path and road by which access can be gained to the cabins — happy thought; plan executed; "pickets" to report first suspicious sound or sight — *entrée*. We were confronted by a roomful of eager, gazing countenances; expressions of surprise, curiosity, wonder, admiration, reverence, joy, and even fear; but "friend" was also stamped on every face. Our admirers appeared dumfounded as they beheld for the first time genuine live Yankees, and observed for the first time rather worn samples of the Yankee blue uniforms casting in relief rows of glittering Federal buttons. Grand fire on the hearth — makes the room appear as light as the day. Indiscreet? Not while trusty "pickets" are guarding every approach. A scent and view of tempting edibles on the hearth made us rather averse to lengthened preliminaries. "Aunt Mary" took the hint, and soon the rustic table groaned with evidences of her sympathy for us and the cause we represented. Sweet bacon, warm wheat-flour biscuits, potatoes, and some homely delicacies that stood well the severe tests we put upon them; nor were we at all abashed by the steadily gazing countenances surrounding us the while.

Supper over, and a "council of war" proposed and held; maps and compass brought into requisition, greatly astonishing our spectators. Anxious inquiries; explanations, in spite of which were uttered blank or indefinite expressions indicative of inability to understand how the Yankees had been able to map out so accurately on cloth this immediate vicinity and the whole country, with its roads, railroads, rivers, cities, and towns. Explanations were insufficient to clear up the mystery. Determining location — twenty-four miles a little east of south from Atlanta. Federal raids had caused the Confederates to closely guard every mill and cross-road of importance in the vicinity. The guards could unite in the defence of any threatened point, and they also served to prevent suspected stampedes of negroes to the Federal lines. Negroes who had recently returned from the "front" reported that the Federals were expected "in these parts 'fore long." The whites, however, professed an opposite opinion. Pronounced decidedly perilous to proceed northward — urged to wait a few days in safety until further news from our friends arrived. The proposition seriously considered; L. votes "aye," strong. Basing action upon the uncertainty of the situation at Atlanta and the certainty of danger ahead, and upon the fact of weariness, — meaning exhaustion, — and the liability of falling into worse keeping, we concluded to remain encamped near by until possessed of further information. The negroes clapped their hands with joy at our decision, promising to render any assistance possible.

It was now after midnight. The question arose as to where the "elephant guests" were to be concealed. We desire no bed. The "straw-house" is settled upon as our resting-place for the remainder of the night. The straw-house was situated on the road, and formed connection with the fence on both sides of it. Peyt and ourselves worked with a will, and as the result a comfortable room was made; and with the aid of rails and planks, walls and ceiling of straw were constructed, all below the surface, yet above the ground. The straw-house was built of hewn logs, which were separated by spaces varying from one-eighth to one-quarter of an inch. We worked passages to the sides of the building through the straw, and thus obtained both light and air. There was also afforded an unobstructed view of the road, upon which we frequently reviewed squads of Confederate cavalry as they passed, — sometimes six, sometimes four or five, and at other times but two. As our place of observation was only a few feet distant from them, we were able to closely inspect them from crown to foot. Their expressions of countenance as well as of voice, their equipments and arms, and even the color of their hair and eyes, were readily noted as they passed unsuspectingly along. After numerous whispered speculations as to the situation and the future, two tired "tramps" slept soundly and sweetly in the comfortable quarters of straw until the dawn of —

August 2. — Road well travelled; quite a military highway. Squads of rebel cavalry pass — look sleepy; must have been on picket all night. They have my earnest sympathy — "been there myself." Forage-wagons, well guarded — citizen horseman. Noon; "black ravens" bring us "dinner," and fill our canteen afresh. Awful hot; perspiration rolling off end of L.'s frontispiece — dripping mortals. Evening's cool shadows; summoned by faithful Peyt to supper — dark. A few trusty sable friends had been intrusted with the "tremendous secret," which accounted for the reverential side-glances of strange colored faces toward the straw-house during the day.

At "Aunt Mary's" cabin again, with the usual precautions of "pickets" guarding every path. What! why, every sacrifice has been made to do us honor. Sweet milk? — what a luxury! Fried chicken? — manna in the desert! A shade of sadness while contemplating that it was Aunt Mary's old pet hen. If we had only known it in advance, would have pleaded for her life; but since it was a *fait accompli* without our knowledge or consent, objections are eminently out of place; wouldn't restore the poor old fowl, to die again, if we had the power. "Please pass the chicken." Oh, flavor exquisite of ancient recollections! Doesn't matter in the least that the recollections of the main subject-matter are more *tender*,— it was never sweeter. After gorging, we chatted pleasantly until near midnight. We soon discovered that, though ignorant, the negroes well understood the nature of the attempt to destroy the Union, and the result of success or defeat of the Federal arms so far as *they* were concerned. What they knew, coupled with what they believed, made a Federal soldier almost an object of worship with them. Retirement to the straw-house; pilot ahead; pickets relieved; sound sleep — sweet rest.

August 3. — More baggage or forage wagons — cavalry; clanking sabres; navy-revolvers. Who knows but that some fine morning or night they'll take a fancy to this straw? Now, why didn't we think of that before? The army is short of every thing, and at any time "Old Shag," as the darkies humorously dubbed Mr. Smith, might be relieved of his straw. Wish we could get out of this. The thoughts of possible demand for straw for hospital or other purposes rendered us exceedingly uncomfortable; then, to think of an ignominious recapture! Faithful

Peyt and dinner (?) — call it lunch, then. After noon Mr. Smith's children came romping down the road, and selected a spot adjoining the straw-house for childish play and prattle — lucky they can't climb up into the straw-house. That light-haired, blue-eyed little girl knew not of the admiring eyes peering at her between the logs of the old straw-house, nor how near she came (the innocent little creature) to a brace of horrid Yankees! Evidently she had been taught to hate "the enemy," though she could not comprehend the meaning of the war, nor realize the significance of the sounds of the great guns before Atlanta. She had nothing to do with mighty principles represented by great armies and heavy artillery. But her cherry lips could part, and the sweet voice of childhood could sing, —

> "Old Lincoln and his hireling troops
> Will never whip the South."

This seemed her favorite song, and often we heard her sweet voice warbling the words. To-night was but a repetition of last night. For the reasons indicated, we concluded to occupy the straw-house only for sleeping purposes, and to retire at dawn to the cool shades of the neighboring woods back of the negro cabins. The programme was executed safely.

August 4. — We spent most of the day in cutting and preparing limbs and saplings, and constructing a double bower-house for our convenience and concealment. We so ingeniously arranged dead limbs around it, that it required very close examination to distinguish it from the veritable brush-pile from which it was largely constructed. The sounds of great guns distinctly heard booming almost incessantly in the direction of Atlanta. [Sherman's long-range guns were shelling the doomed city.] At intervals we also heard rumblings as if of musketry, but it couldn't have been at Atlanta — probably some raiding party nearer us. Accompanying the "music in the air," is an unusual excitement. The roads are filled with the teams of frightened refugees, who, with families and effects, are seeking places of safety. "What does all this commotion mean?" The terror of the natives was necessarily our joy — cruel, perhaps, but we could not control the circumstances which so fixed the facts. Inquiries made during the night failed to account for the agitation of the day.

August 5. — Bower-house quite an improvement on straw. We began to grow courageous, fat, and restless — foraging expedition, resulting in gathering of luscious blackberries. At noon we were honored by the appearance of Aunt Mary in proper person, laden with a bountiful supply of warm corn bread and cow-peas. Calm, beautiful day. Most of our time was employed in watching two little wrens, who heeded not the distinction between the "blue and the gray," and who appeared to occasionally hesitate and wonder at the mysterious, heavy sounds of war in the distance. At times they would approach us, limb by limb, from above, until almost within reach; turning their little heads, first one side, then the other, toward us, peering at us with a suspicious, inquiring gaze, their tiny black eyes scintillating in the sunlight. They were apparently well pleased with our compliments and flatteries. After thoroughly inspecting our "nest," they busied themselves beautifying and completing their own; and all day long it was work and sing — work and sing. Perhaps there's no lesson to be learned from such an observation — perhaps superiority lies with the inferior creature. To work and *fret* seems to be the peculiar tendency of man.

August 6. — Very early this morning we were awakened by faithful Peyt with "Wake up, gemmen! Do you hear that noise? De devil is to pay dis mornin'!" And sure enough, the rapid peals of artillery, rapidly increasing to a continuous roar, and just at daybreak, indicated that something extraordinary or unexpected had occurred; and our expectations were not lessened by the fact that before sunrise all firing had ceased, and silence became as ominous as was the thunder which preceded it. We anxiously awaited tidings from the road and from the front, but waited in vain, and finally concluded that there had been some reason unknown to us why our guns should thunder an extra morning salute to the enemy. We rambled through the thick woods for much-needed exercise. Visitors called upon us to-day — several negroes (leaders) from adjoining plantations, many of whom had come a great distance to see live Yankees; expressions of sympathy and loyalty; true friends. The colored delegation silently depart, after gratifying their curiosity; wishing us God-speed, and encouraging us to keep up our "sperits." Later in the afternoon an old dog belonging to some of the negroes, called "Old Buck," scented mystery in the air, and slowly wound his way to our bower-house; and seeming to have solved the cause of the mysterious movements of his master and friends, sensibly withdrew as silently as they.

While ensconced in the woods in rear of Smith's plantation, our main dependencies were she whom all called "Aunt Mary," and her brother "Peyt." Aunt Mary is medium in size, rather slender in figure, and black as the night. Gentle and kind, and unable to do too much for her guests, — of whom she has voluntarily assumed the especial care; jealous of the attentions of others; "willing to work her hands off;" an excellent cook. Her husband is a slave on a neighboring plantation, and is permitted to *call* on her semi-occasionally. Shrewd when occasion calls for it; affectionate — very fond of her children; says she "thinks as much of us as if we were her own chile;" does the milking for her master's family — knows how to obtain enough milk for us, and yet leave the usual *quantity* for the family; continually mindful of our interests; generous and sensible. "Peyt," "own brother to Aunt Mary," is medium size, stout; untiring in his efforts to please and cheer us — swears by what we say; shrewd, agile, and expert with a *rock* — can knock a hog down with a rock, in the dark, at an incredible distance, and cut its throat before it recovers — likes a big secret, and also gazes wistfully at my watch — seems slightly jealous of our civilities to other visiting field-hands — entertains us by relating his wonderful escapes from snakes and blood-hounds — knows all about fishes — bold and kind, attentive and true.

Our bower-house was a model in its style, and so constructed as to present to every approach the appearance of a veritable *brush-heap;* the entrance was a winding approach, to carry out the deception. But alas! with all of our nicety of calculation we had failed to render it storm-proof, as was demonstrated this very night. Just at the close of day, huge dark clouds obscured the sunlight, and soon after, the storm burst upon us in sudden fury! Rain fell in torrents; the wind howled fearfully through the forest, and even the aged oaks bent their heads to the fury of the gale. Our slender "fortifications" were speedily swept away, and strewn in shapeless *débris* about the woods. We were summarily "wet to the buff," and driven through the deluge to the rear door of Aunt Mary's protecting hut. She was expecting us, and, as we approached, her hospitable door opened to welcome us. Drenched; huge hearth-fire; wringing out — drying. A bit of news is related to us during the process. A considerable body of Confederate troops encamped near us to-day. Confederate soldiers visited Smith's plantation, and desired to purchase chickens, etc. Sagacious Aunt Mary inquired about particulars, and ascertained that they would "move on" to-night. Their presence caused some excitement and extra precautions on our part. Near midnight the question arose, "Where shall we sleep?" In the woods? — dripping wet. In the straw-house? — particularly unsafe. Aunt Mary declared we should not sleep uncomfortable again, so long as she had quilts in her cabin. She furnished us with sufficient bedding, and we constructed a pallet on the floor of the loft of the cabin, and sweetly slept until the dawn of —

August 7. — We were awakened by the voice of our hostess, calling in a loud whisper from below, "Hi, hi! Look out on de road." We peeped through apertures, and there they were! We counted thirty-five "butternuts," well mounted and armed, passing leisurely along the road eastwardly toward the Confederate right flank — not an unusual occurrence, and need not be accounted for. Around us are evidences of the severity of last evening's storm, but "Old Sol" shines out this morning as if in surprise at the wrecks of the past night. Breakfast; retreat to the woods; demolished habitation. How much skill and labor are required to reinstate our "residence" in our affections! Let's see; if our calculations are correct, this day must be Sunday — beautiful, clear, and calm. Listen! no sounds save the sweet warbling of feathered friends and the tinkling bells on peaceful, distant pastures. Friends — home! How many are hoping and fearing on our account to-day? How much or how little do they know concerning us? Do they think us alive, or dead? We are indeed lost to each other; hope alone encourages. Thoughts of church, of people, of hymns, of familiar scenery, of childhood's scenes and events. Supreme luxury afforded by reading from leaves of old books found in the loft where we "roosted" last night. Here comes Aunt Mary and attendants, laden with luxuries for our enjoyment. Chicken-pie! ye gods, think of that! fried corn, and excellent corn bread — a repast for a king. Refreshments; thanks. Sunset — flood of golden light streaming through the foliage — exquisite beauty; all nature seems bathing —

> "In the golden lightning
> Of the sunken sun."

August 8. — *Ennui* — spirit for adventure — nerve for encounter; impatience. Peyt suggests that writer "go a-fishing "— agreed; the writer dons Peyt's old hat and old gray coat, and provided with hook and line, under Peyt's guidance, was soon at " Cotton Indian Creek." Peyt returned, leaving the writer patiently fishing — patience reaps reward; net result, four small catfish and one mammoth eel — the latter seriously objected to capture. After being fairly landed, he broke the hook and made for the water. The writer seized the prize, and a closely contested struggle ensued. Slipping from one grasp to another, the "enemy" gained the water's edge. Hands, boots, fish-line, and pole were brought into requisition, and the monster was rethrown upon the bank and forced to submit to "unconditional surrender;" it was demonstrated, however, that victory is not always to the "slippery" — glory enough for the first excursion. The useful remnants of the struggle were gathered with the "vanquished foe," and, covered with the glory and "slime" of conflict, the writer beat a safe retreat to his "headquarters." Eel and catfish for the closing meal of the day.

August 9. — Fishing is now in vogue; both L. and the writer fish in the creek to-day. We caught no fish, but were ourselves caught in a heavy shower of rain — again "wet to the buff;" return; welcome — drying-out; slept soundly on the forge of the blacksmith-shop near by. Peyt appears with the daylight of —

August 10, — Warning us that "de mornin's yere." L. and the writer again venture fishing — Confederate fish seem to scorn our efforts; we return at mid-day, fishless and fish-hookless. Aunt Mary's negro boy Wash awaited us, with dinner, and Aunt Mary's regrets that it was the best she had. Wash is about fifteen, and seems never so happy as when he can secure our attention to listen to his knowledge concerning, and experiences with, "snakes." He seems to think that he has "rights," in the absence of the old folks, which we are bound to respect, and give him a patient hearing. We slightly encourage him, and while we eat we listen attentively to the boy's dissertation on land and water moccasins and his hair-breadth escapes from their poisonous fangs. Wash eyes us intently the while, evidently eager to detect the slightest indication of incredulity; but we are all ears and wonderment! Not even the most extravagant stretch can cause even a knowing look to pass between us, and Wash retires, manifestly convinced that we are solemnly impressed with his heroism. Usual evening meeting and greeting. A night's rest in the friendly deserted blacksmith-shop — broken, however, by the bellowing great guns in the north. Our guns were serenading Atlanta all night. Sherman is before that doomed city, by night as well as by day. Maybe something unusual has happened to cause the unusual night cannonade. The first indications of daylight brought the reliable Peyt to our "bed," to warn us to retreat early to a place of safety.

August 11. — Retreat to the bower in the woods. The path through the woods was well commanded from our innocent-looking "brush-pile," and while carelessly looking in that direction, the writer saw approaching a *white man in Confederate uniform!* Flat! flat on the ground — eyes fixed on the approaching soldier. He carelessly advances — is now abreast — notices nothing — breathless we; he's past — tally one for the "brush-pile" — he carries a fish-pole and basket, and is bound for the creek — our fishing is over. "Who could that be?" It must be he whom the negroes speak of as "Corporal Sid," Mr. Smith's son, home on furlough from the front. How pale and ghastly he looked — furlough well granted. We must keep "in-doors" and be all eyes and ears until his return — disappointed — he returned another way. Aunt Mary appeared with *eels* for supper. "Who caught them?" "Corporal Sid, to-day." The mystery explained; conjectures correct. "I reckoned it would be so queer for you 'uns to be a-eaten fish cotched by Corporal Sid," said Aunt Mary, with a merry laugh — good joke. Demonstrated that catching by blue or gray does not alter the *flavor* of eels — strictly non-partisan — neutral and impartial, yet *slippery* and unreliable — squirms like a politician. And now, Corporal Sid, if the statute of limitations has not barred your claim, charge us for "fried eels."

We are made to feel that we are indeed guests, by

being informed that a grand jubilee is to be held to-night in our honor — the only entertainment possible. Early evening — guests silently gather. Owing to the presence of two negroes who are ignorant of our presence, and who are not known to be trustworthy, and who have "big mouths" (talk too much), we conclude to secretly observe the "performance," concealed in a patch of sugar-corn — good view — bonfire — all in their best — mouth music — fantastic motions — profuse perspiration — earnestness — interest — carried away — joy unconfined and beyond control — general excitement; every muscle in action, young and old — "glory! glory!". Genuine, glorious jubilee — no counterfeit of the stage can equal or truly depict this. This is not for the enjoyment of *audiences*, but for the participants only. Therein is the main difference between the genuine and the imitation. The genuine enjoyment evidenced by motions, sounds, songs, and features cannot be successfully feigned — rare treat; thanks for the honor — to our trusty friends a secret and silent "good-night."

We slept soundly away into the night, when the writer was awakened by L.'s elbow vigorously applied to his side, with "Just listen at that!" "At what?" asked the writer, half rising. "Listen," said L., while the air seemed filled with the dull, heavy sounds of Sherman's artillery! We listened and conjectured. Was it a night attack? Was Sherman or Hood attacking? How we yearn for a sight of the blue-coats. Listen! the distant thunder of heavy guns — midnight's slumbers broken by dreaded rumblings of war; but the cannon's echo, that awakens, grows again familiar and lulls to sleep. Break of day.

August 12. — Timely calling, and retreat to the woods! Cloudy again, —
> "It seems like yesterday come back
> With its old things, and not to-day."

Armed with poles, hooks, and lines, and being assured of Corporal Sid's confining illness, we determined again to try our luck fishing, and cautiously repaired to the creek. We had been at the creek but a short time when Peyt, like a grim, dark spectre, suddenly emerged from the thick foliage, and with trembling voice and protruding eyeballs imparted the information that the Confederate cavalry had just notified Mr. Smith (his master) that the Yankees would be upon him to-day! Great excitement prevailed; valuables were being speedily concealed — whites trembling with fear — negroes wild with ill-concealed delight — valuables will be concealed in the woods, and "brush-piles" invite patronage — unsafe and imprudent to return to our retreat; we remain here; Peyt to proceed to the "front" (plantation), and apprise us of any change in present *status* — agreed — congratulations at prospect of soon being "captured" by the blue-coats! Premature rejoicing — the day flies, the *status* remains unchanged. The evening comes, and disappointment's mist surrounds us; at dark we return to our bower, spend the evening in allaying excitement and enjoining caution, and sleep in the woods till the dawn of —

Saturday, August 13.—We are informed that Saturdays are days generally selected by old men and boys for fishing. Accordingly, we abandon the idea of fishing to-day, and quietly remain "at home." We are also apprised of reasons for extra precautions. Encamped in the woods near us is the family of a refugee named Darby. In fleeing from the Yankees, he brought, with other personal property, his slaves, among them three boys (male slaves are all "boys"). The boys have failed to report at the camp, and are rated as runaways. The "young bloods" of this community — the "stay-at-homes" — have organizations for the purpose of keeping the negroes in subjection, and of rendering mutual assistance in reducing to the possession of the master strayed "personal property." These gentlemen are styled by the negroes "patrollers," from the fact that they act as a patrol-guard from plantation to plantation, and generally at night. Objects of terror to the negroes — strange stories of useless violence and brutality — sometimes masked. We are earnestly warned that they will probably scour the woods for runaways to-night, and perhaps search the cabins — frequent occurrence; dilemma — council of war; plan: let there be a jubilee, to invite the attention of the patrollers from the woods to the cabins — we know not in which direction lies safety. Night — our position taken in a thin patch of sugar-corn near the scene of the jubilee, to see and not be seen. The jubilee; sounds of revelry — other suspicious sounds in the edges of the woods — all ears to the rear — cracking of dry limbs — stealthy footfalls — forms appear; outlines just visible through the darkness — now we see, crouching and gliding toward the scene of merriment, three human forms — now, with demoniac yells, they charge into the crowd of happy negroes. The "boys," or "bucks," scatter like chaff before the wind, amid cries of "Halt! halt!" "Shoot him! shoot him!" etc. Flat on the ground we, twenty feet distant, and silent and motionless as fallen statues — the women alone remained, and mutely received the oaths and curses lavishly launched at their race in general, and at the runaways in particular. A few "bucks" were clubbed in the *mêlée*, but the abuse of the women was only verbal. "Where was Mr. Smith, the master of the plantation?" The answer we obtained was that the "right of search," with its concomitant brutalities, was a sort of common courtesy extended for mutual protection of kindred interests. The runaways were at the jubilee, but were continually on the *qui vive*, and off like the wind at the first suspicious sound. The patrollers hold a hurried consultation, and depart; we cautiously retreat toward the bower-house in the woods; we suddenly came upon a fancily attired darkey, a stranger, who, upon our approach, bounded off through the woods like a frightened deer!

Faithful Peyt cautiously overtakes and informs us that the patrollers were "Mr. Darby and two young gemmen" (stay-at-homes) — that the danger is now passed. We proceed cautiously by starlight toward the bower; approach it — suddenly we discover, lying behind a fallen tree, three human forms, evidently awaiting our approach. We stood as if petrified! Retreat? Impossible! Now seemed a revelation of the truth — the plan and object was to *trap us*, not the negroes. There lay the three armed trappers — with all of our pains, that the end should come to this — trapped at last! At last the forms move — heads are elevated. Will they fire without a word? Will they demand our surrender? Delay gives hope. What if their faces are black? Three—ominous number; yet no sound, but we *feel* their gaze fixed on us — recurring question: "Black or white?" Impulse to speak, but — one step nearer, and heads are suddenly thrown up, and we meet the curious gaze of three *black* faces! Upon the color of those features depended at least our safety, perhaps our lives. But the mystery is yet unsolved: three *strangers!* We hail, confer, congratulate — Darby's runaways; more terrified than we — they had heard of us through Peyt. It did not take much argument to convince these "boys" that our safety required their immediate return to their master. They promised faithfully to do so on the morrow — secrecy enjoined and promised — departure. We reached the bower in rather a fretted state of mind, but sleep remained a stranger to us until near the dawn of —

August 14. — Sunday again. "All quiet along the lines." One of our black "scouts" brings information that the three "patrollers" held a conference this morning on the road near the cabins; this information set us thinking. Have the runaways returned? What if *bloodhounds* should be brought into requisition? "Return, O prodigals, return!" Grave suspicions—can it be possible that we have been discovered or betrayed? Are the "patrollers" after *white* game, instead of black? Uncomfortable suggestions. Toward evening, through an abundance of caution, Aunt Mary brought us our "dinner and supper together." All is subdued excitement on the plantation — she cautiously winds her way back to her cabin. Dark — we approach the cabin very cautiously, but are met and warned by a friendly "scout" that the three patrollers of the evening before are at this moment in Aunt Mary's cabin! Why is this? Suspicions strengthened — white game — we have been betrayed or discovered — military necessity to hear subject of conversation — writer nears the cabin and listens. Aunt Mary is catching a severe lecture on the general behavior of negroes — nothing more — suspicions weakened; "scout" remains to watch and report movements of the dreaded trio, and we retreat to the bower, and each alternately watches and rests, not to say sleep. Grave apprehensions and well-founded anxieties are not conducive to healthy slumber.

August 15. — Fishing — splendid mess from somebody's fish-basket or trap. Rest rendered sweeter by information that Darby's "boys" have returned to him.

August 16. — Fish-basket empty; L. suggests that the fish know that the Yankees set the trap. Oh, for a miniature Confederate flag as a decoy! Our ears are regaled by sudden bursts of artillery-fire directly westward! [It was Gen. Kilpatrick's cavalry raiding at Lovejoy's Station, on the Atlanta and Macon Railroad.]

August 17. — Fishing, but fishless. At the cabin at dusk; precaution taken to post, from seventy to eighty yards from the cabin, on every approach, negro urchins, while little negro girls hovered around the cabin to catch and convey to us the first alarm — trusty, watchful pickets. We had just seated ourselves at "supper," when in came the little picket that had been stationed at the road-fence, or gate, and excitedly informed us that "de patrollers" were silently sneaking up toward the path along the fence on the road! We silently and cautiously retreat to the woods — conference. What could this mean? Darby's boys returned, and the "patrollers" still out! Have Darby's boys betrayed us to shield themselves? Bowerhouse untenable — utmost caution guards our every movement — we select a position distant from the bower retreat, yet commanding it, and at least one pair of eyes bore upon it through the dim starlight of the long night. No approach, no report, no development — puzzling anxiety.

August 18. — We learn that the "patrollers" quietly inspected the cabins and departed, speechless. Apprehensions growing. Our plan is utmost caution, and awaiting developments. Fishing alone. To doff the blue and don the gray will make a bolder fisherman. Done! Peyt's old gray coat accepted and worn. At the creek. Discovery — a fish-pole rises and falls over the stream a short distance above; the holder screened in the thick foliage which lines the creek — curiosity to see this encroaching fisherman. His pole is withdrawn, and supposing the holder will pass down on the opposite side of the stream, the writer selects a concealed position and anxiously awaits the "passing in review." Sharp crack of a limb behind — the writer turns, and there stands the awaited personage, accompanied by a boy and a large dog, all steadily gazing at the writer. Fairly caught! They had crossed the creek, and descended on the *wrong* side. Fifty feet between us — to speak would encourage accent to belie the gray coat — to advance, folly — to run would betray. Hardly knowing what to do, the writer calmly put his hands in his pockets, and walked off in rather a careless manner, whistling the "Bonnie Blue Flag," almost unconsciously turning to witness the effect of the movement. There stood the trio, with gaze still fixed on the whistler. The man — a heavy, thick-set, corpulent, red-faced gent — now handed the boy his pole, and deliberately rolled up his shirt-sleeves (he was coatless). What does he mean by that? He must be as frightened as the writer! Does he mean "fight?" "Can't see it — there is no occasion for personal encounter." Whistling and retreat continue. Direction of retreat is away from the bower, but as soon as the foliage concealed the writer's form, he circled around and reached his goal unobserved. Extra vigilance, however, was maintained throughout the night, on account of the writer's experience at the creek.

After dark, Peyt appeared and induced the writer to accompany him on a raid to a plantation some two miles distant — object, to "forage on the enemy." Agreed. The silent night-march; the ripe watermelon patch — luscious; grand peach-orchard. After eating to our entire satisfaction, we filled ready pillow-slips for the benefit of "the loved ones at home." *En route* homeward, we rested under a friendly oak which graced the centre of a large pasture, and being exhausted by *internal* and external burdens, we were soon in deep slumber. When we awoke, we were at first surprised to view the numerous pairs of glistening eyes surrounding us. The pets of the pasture had discovered us, and horses and mules vied with each other in making near approaches to the objects of their curiosity. At a given signal, we suddenly arose, and the panic that ensued created a realization of our indiscretion. Repetitions of the sport developed that quadrupeds and bipeds alike enjoy fun. Arise! Take burdens! March! Shortly after midnight we arrive at the only place we can call "home."

August 19. — Fishing excursions unpopular; spent most of the day recovering from the effort of last night. At night the western sky seemed ablaze! We guess the Yankees must be at work near Jonesboro, only twelve miles distant. Pursuant to arrangement of Peyt, a strange negro, named "Jim," presented himself to us as a pilot to conduct my companion, L., to the Federal lines. With or without cause, and unknown to L., both Peyt and Aunt Mary had expressed themselves as unwilling to risk themselves further on L.'s account. Rightfully or wrongfully, they accused him of many acts of indiscretion, which created alarm lest he should be discovered and they severely dealt with. One offence was his careless approach to the cabin by daylight, which caused some questions to be asked by some of Mr. Smith's family, who saw him. In addition to this, L. seemed rather diffident, and took no pains to please or instruct our hosts; and the original interest which they took in him wearing away, without replacement, seemed to have its effect; nor could they accept the excuse of youth for acts of indiscretion imperilling their own safety. Personally, the writer makes not a single complaint against L. The negroes had simply lost confidence in him, which they could not regain, and argument seemed powerless to restore it. L. was persuaded to go, however, and Jim and L. started together for the Federal lines. Expectations of the Federal advance, and continued illness of the writer, permitted the separation. "Farewell, L., and may you get through safely. Who gets through first, must bear the messages of the other. Good-bye." L. had scarcely got beyond hailing-distance, when the writer regretted that he had not accompanied him — lonely. The writer selected new quarters to sleep: Uncle Davie's shoe-shop, in rear of the cabins.

August 20. — Retreat to the old bower at daylight. Shortly after, great excitement reigns. "The Yankees are coming! the Yankees are coming!" is the report. Upon urgent appeal, the writer quickly glided into Aunt

Mary's cabin, and up into the loft, where through an aperture he could watch the road. Patiently watching — no Yankees. While thus engaged, one of the fair residents of the mansion, or "big house," came to Aunt Mary's cabin and deposited with her a bundle of letters and photographs for safe-keeping, in the common belief that the Federals never searched negroes. This, the writer learned, was a widow lady, named Mrs. Stancil. While visiting the cabin she related to Aunt Mary a "queer dream," to which the writer listened attentively. It was an adventure with a "Federal captain" (one bar beyond my rank). The charming widow sat directly beneath the writer, on Aunt Mary's bed, and by peering through the open flooring, a fair "bird's-eye view" was obtained. The fair lady suddenly threw herself back upon the bed and gazed directly upward! It seemed that our glances met instantly! To move would certainly attract her attention. The lady dreamily inspected the board ceiling above her, and the writer remained a fixed prisoner until relieved by the presence of mind of Aunt Mary, who, feigning to desire some article of bed-clothing, forced the lady to a sitting posture. Shortly after, she returned as she came. The special deposit of photographs and love-letters were handed to the writer. The letters were from a lieutenant in the Confederate army, and their contents — are not "contraband of war."

Rather late in the afternoon there were discovered on

the road rebel pickets, mounted, passing eastwardly, stating to Mr. Smith that they had been "driven in by the Yankees, who were immediately behind and coming on." Then followed a scene of hurried confusion! Mr. Smith and his son, Corporal Sid, with the field-hands and family valuables, beat a hasty retreat to a neighboring swamp. The trembling ladies and children were left in the house to meet the foe. Aunt Mary had in her wash-tub all the underclothes the writer possessed. They were speedily extracted therefrom, hastily wrung and passed up, and, in the emergency, pulled on — wet. The negroes had been told to "run for their lives;" but there was an influence the whites could not understand, which caused them to instinctively cluster around the cabin of Aunt Mary, calmly awaiting the appearance of the blue-coats. Anxious eyes were fixed steadily on the road over which the Confederate pickets had just been driven, and the watch was kept long and eagerly. No dust — no appearance — night drawing near — impatience. Suddenly the booming of cannon is heard; direction — south of west; not *three miles* away! As we suspected, the column had left our road only three miles west of us, and was now proceeding to McDonough, Georgia, which was three miles southward. The Yankees are shelling the rebel pickets that dispute the passage to the town — the dispute is short, and the Federal raiders pass through the town, and return to the Federal lines at Covington,

Georgia, thus completing a circuit around us, and within *three miles* of lending us joy supreme! Bitter disappointment; bleeding hopes — blank despondency! In the slightest hope that perhaps a few blue-coats might ramble to this plantation for food or forage, the writer permitted his spirits to droop in Aunt Mary's loft all night.

August 21. — The atmosphere is thick with rumors, but no Yankees appear. At the bower in the woods; lonesome — no reports; no consolation — alone. At night, "Jim," who had started for our lines with L., returned with bitter complaints that L. was "clumsy" and indiscreet. He reported that, on the first day out, L. insisted on raiding a melon-patch by daylight, against J.'s protest and warning, and was seen by the owner of the plantation, Mr. Gleaton. From some of Gleaton's negroes Jim learned that Gleaton had reported the circumstance of a man in blue in his melon-patch, to the Confederate cavalry! Howbeit, Jim refused to accompany L. further, turned him over to other friendly negroes, and returned, and begged leave to guide the writer to the Federal lines. This was agreed to, on condition that Jim should proceed to plantations on the line of the recent raid, and gather all the information possible concerning the raiders, and the *status* at Atlanta, and return; while the writer determined to interview Mr. Smith as to what he knew, from reports of the Confederate cavalry who had daily passed his door. With this understanding, Jim departed. The writer conferred with Peyt and Aunt Mary, and astounded both by declaring, "I am going to talk with Mr. Smith and his family this night." In vain were the warnings of danger and deceit; but upon solemn assurances that dangerous visiting relatives were in the house, the interview was postponed one day. The writer had been well informed that Mr. Smith was a strong Southern man, imbued with strong prejudices against any thing blue; had a son in the Confederate army, who is now at home, and the whole family enthusiastic in the Southern cause; but by mere accident he also obtained information of the fact that Mr. Smith was a prominent member of a fraternity which is worldwide in extent, and which has survived all wars and civil strife, and by means of which "enemies" meet as "brothers." On the fly-leaf of an old book a note was written to Mr. Smith apprising him of the presence of a Federal officer, and claiming also to be a brother in distress, and desiring information regarding his friends, and attaching the mystic sign of the order. Every thing now awaited —

August 23. — As the writer was about to enter the bower-retreat, the rustling of leaves within revealed the presence of a prior occupant in the shape of a huge black-snake, who seemed willing to contest his right of entry. A well-directed blow at the head of the black intruder, with the hickory cane the writer always carried, but which his snakeship artfully dodged, caused him to glide through the rustic confines of the bower and rapidly away through the shrubbery. Evening — the plan was announced for the attempt on the "big house" to-night. The house-dog to be secured, and retained in one of the cabins — pickets selected to watch the road, and to cast a pebble against the window should cavalry halt at the gate. The slave "Charlie" was selected to be hailed by the writer on the road and deliver the note to Mr. Smith. This programme was executed, and when Charlie rapped at the front-door, the writer had taken a position near by, where he could hear the conversation within through the open window. Charlie told his story of being hailed on the road by a stranger and requested to deliver the note to his master and await an answer. Charlie was ordered to wait. The door was closed, and one of the ladies read the note aloud. Corporal Sid, who had retired, was aroused, and a long and wordy conference followed, in hushed accents. A note was returned to Charlie, who was informed that the "stranger" who had hailed him was a *Yankee!* Charlie feigned great surprise, and returned, with seeming reluctance, with the answer. The substance of the answer was: "Although an enemy, yet, if you are what you profess to be, you will not be harmed at my house. My son is home sick from the Confederate army; but you can meet in peace. at my house, even if you cannot elsewhere." Signed, "Smith."

Aunt Mary and Peyt were assured that, whatever happened, nothing should compromise or implicate them. Charlie guided me to the front gate, where Mr. Smith stood to receive me. Greeting; hand-shaking; mysterious questions, promptly answered — expressions of satisfaction — invitation to "come in" accepted — *entrée*. There sat in waiting three ladies — Mrs. Stancil was immediately recognized as one. Mr. Smith politely introduced the writer as a "Federal officer" to his ladies and to his son Sidney. They had never before seen a "Federal," nor a Federal uniform, and both seemed objects of great curiosity — but all seemed also to realize that before them stood the representative of a hated idea! The writer's first remark, after raising his fatigue cap, was, "You see, ladies, that we do not wear horns;" but manifestly they were in no humorous mood.

Mr. Smith engaged the writer in friendly conversation about lodges, the war, armies, Atlanta, Sherman, Hood, etc., growing rather vehement, and exclaiming, "I tell you, sir, the Yankees can *never* take Atlanta — *never!*" The writer replied, "Well, we differ there. If you knew the character of our Western army and its commander, you would never expect to see them go backwards. Atlanta *must fall*, sir." The old gentleman simply bit his lip, as if half believing it. The ladies, now becoming more social, ventured to ask the writer numerous questions, until the conversation became quite general, changing into a brisk chat between the heroine of the cabin, Mrs. Stancil, and the writer, to which the others seemed content to listen. How the mention of a *circumstance* would cause her surprise! how the mention of a *name* would bring her to her feet! "Have you many friends in the rebel — Confederate army, Mrs. Stancil?" "A few," she responded. "And none in our army?" "None," was the reply.

The writer now turned his attention to the other object of secret admiration, — the "Corporal Sid." Gray uniform — brass buttons; corporal's chevrons — sullen features — arms folded — standing — looks upon the present scene as though he entertained grave doubts as to its propriety — reluctant assent — compromise - of - dignity air; entertaining a Yankee — probably jealous of writer's attention to others; Confederate military importance slighted — gray snubbed by the blue in its own stronghold. The corporal closely scans the uniform of the writer — dark blue — eagle buttons — staff shoulder-straps — well-worn staff trimmings — sky-blue welts on outer seam of pants; worse for wear; military boots — within them all an unrestrained enemy! We will raise no question of *rank*, but if there is to be one, since it can avail nothing and effect nothing, let it be conceded that, under the circumstances, *chevrons* on gray outrank *straps* on blue. Now to force an "engagement" with the enemy in hostile uniform. "Sorry you are so sick, sir, and unable to participate in the fun at the front." "Yaas, sorry too," was the response. Slowly and cautiously the conversation continued — answers, for the most part, in monosyllables. Now the corporal warms to the conversation, and ventures to explain the difference between "ou' armee an' you' armee" by the presence in the latter of a great *foreign* element. The writer ventured the remark that that fact possibly enured to the credit of the foreigners, and to the discredit of natives opposing them. (Wonder if he saw the point?) Guard against personalities — remember the situation — no place to discuss war issues — danger can appear at the wave of a hand!

Now Mr. Smith reënters from the dining-room, and politely said to the writer, "I have ordered supper for you, and it is all ready, sir; will you step out?" A flash of *suspicion*— unfounded, perhaps, but still entertained — no reason for it, but nevertheless felt — superabundance of caution, perhaps. Howbeit, it moved the lips to say, "Had I known of the preparation, I should have stopped it; having partaken heartily before I came, I must ask you to accept my thanks, and excuse me." "If you insist upon it," said Mr. Smith. "And now it is so late, you had better remain with us the balance of the night." Thoughts. Was the *bed* to accomplish what the table could not? Where is the element of trust? Why abuse kindness without reason? — faithful guards are on duty, why decline? "I am so weary, sir, and worn, that I accept your kindness for the remainder of the night." A candle — a pleasant good-night to all. Mr. Smith conducts the writer to bed-chamber on first floor — the nearer to my "guards" I sleep, the better I shall feel. Will they understand this movement? "Goodnight, stranger." "Good-night, sir;" and the door was closed and locked. Comfortable, soft bed. Who says that one enured to hardships cannot rest on feathers, *lies* not on feathers, but under a mistake.

"Weariness can snore upon the flint."

Then why not upon the feathers? Mosquitoes — reason enough; slumbers somewhat disturbed by winged serenaders — assassins of the night; also by troublesome mental inquiries. What if Confederate cavalry stop for information, or breakfast? What if my host send information to them? By whom? By a slave? They are all enlisted in my behalf — rest in the consciousness that "pickets" are faithful and true, and that any evil attempt, or presence of danger, will be promptly communicated by the pebble against the pane — slumber. It may at first blush seem questionable conduct in accepting the hospitality of one whose house was guarded by his own slaves, and the host's family under suspicion, but a close analysis of the situation reveals the affair in its true light.

The hospitality, beyond a mere visit, was not anticipated. Mr. Smith was bound only to the extent of his note, and seemed careful in conversation not to commit himself further. In it the writer is recognized as "an enemy;" but on account of being also a "brother," "will not be harmed at my house." No friendship expressed, no protection, no aid offered, no information given; Mr. Smith might remain true to his word, and the writer be betrayed and seized immediately upon leaving the house; and as he had only one trial at *mistakes*, the caution which only demonstrated Mr. Smith's trustworthiness was considered well taken. But even under ordinary circumstances the distinction is keenly felt between being merely *tolerated* and being welcomed. Doubtless both felt that it was a difficult feat to reconcile the brother with the enemy. During the night there were noises in the house indicating that all were not asleep, and that the writer was not the only one under the roof who was suffering from apprehensions.

August 24. — At daylight a sharp tapping on the window aroused the writer, who arose, to discover that it was only Mr. Smith, apprising of the approach of day. Dressing — appearance — conference. "I desire to go north." Carefully crossing the road, Mr. Smith expresses fear that the "Confederate folks" may be coming along. Piloted on a path by Mr. S., northward, nearly a mile. "Now, if you will remain here awhile," said Mr. S., "I'll send or bring you some breakfast." "Thanks, but time is precious, and I'll move on to thicker cover." Smith accepts thanks for kindness and secrecy, and returns. The writer performed a three-mile circuit, ending at the welcome bower in rear of Aunt Mary's cabin. Tedious march through the dew-wet shrubbery. Wearied and anxious, the writer fell asleep, and within his embrace was a large watermelon which he had gathered *en route*. Luscious bedfellow! He was awakened by the presence of Aunt Mary, who knew of his intention to return and keep his engagement with Jim, and who stood ready with a fine warm breakfast. No suspicion — no fears — no misgivings — no reservations; but perfect confidence. "Ah, how strong is my trust in black!" While the writer eagerly discussed comforts, to which he knew he was heartily welcome, Aunt Mary humorously related the reports of the previous evening's experiences. The mysterious visitor was referred to in terms rather complimentary than otherwise. "Siss," a fair, grown daughter of Mr. Smith, said "he was dressed in Yankee blue from tip to toe." The sweet little miss whom the writer had observed from the straw-house, in her childish innocence and imagination confidentially told Aunt Mary that "his breast was full of pistols!" Mrs. Stancil confessed that she "was very much pleased with the little Yankee officer." (How about that Confederate lieutenant?) She was probably thinking of the Confederate when she added, "I really fell in love with him." Mr. Smith said he was "a gay, bold young Yankee, armed to the teeth;" and gave it as his opinion that "he had plenty of company near at hand." The negroes were all delighted with the adventure, but looked significantly at each other when informed that Smith possessed no information about the armies, although the newspapers were delivered daily at his door. Reports came that during the day there had been unusual passing of cavalry and refugees on the road, and several soldiers had conversed with Mr. Smith, who seemed somewhat excited. The writer's curiosity was also excited. What's the news? All silent Atlantaward. What can it mean? Desperation makes one bold — determination to *squeeze* some information from Smith. At night the writer approached from the north, and hailed at the gate. "What's wanting?" inquired the sweet voice of Siss. "The man of the house," was the response. "Pa," she called, "somebody for you." Mr. S. came to the gate, and the writer explained that he observed extra commotion on the road, and, before starting north, took the liberty to learn from him what news had been brought to him from the front; and that the writer took this method in order not to disturb the peace of his family by reappearance within. Mr. Smith expressed thanks for prudence, and replied, "They all say that Hood has made up his mind to hold Atlanta at all hazards." "Thanks," said the writer, "my course is determined." (It was, to round the Confederate right flank into our lines — useless to wait longer.) The ladies now appeared at the front-door, and peered suspiciously out into the darkness. "They're all excitement again," said Smith. "I'll allay it," replied the writer, "by pretending I am trying to purchase apples of you," and uttered a loud remark to that effect; to which Smith loudly replied, "Yes, sir; but I'm sorry, sir, but apples are very scarce this year;" and the writer passed away in the darkness, silently contemplating the marvellous *dread* of blue cloth. A short circuit again brought him to the bower-house, where he restlessly remained all night.

August 25. — Fishing; thinking; planning; waiting for Jim's return. Anxious to start for the Union lines. Where is that Jim?

August 26. — Occasional booming of a single gun in the direction of Atlanta; irregular and slow firing; indications that they are tired of it. After dark, there suddenly bursts forth a furious cannonade; rapid firing; puzzling!

August 27. — Great excitement! Confederate cavalry report that "Sherman is falling back to the Chattahoochee!" Driven back from Atlanta — repulsed — failure? Whites jubilant; negroes sorrowful; writer nonplussed. "Don't believe it." True or false, time is precious. "Where is Jim?"

Sunday, August 28. — Very early this morning, Jim appeared, with questionable explanations of his absence, and announced himself ready to depart with the writer for the Federal lines. We spend the day arranging our plans and receiving reports of jubilant rebel cavalrymen passing the "big house" and exchanging congratulations with Mr. Smith on account of the "glorious Confederate victory and Yankee defeat!" Ominous silence in the direction of Atlanta seems confirmatory of the report. Negroes much depressed — writer unable to explain — situation puzzling. What! "defeat?" The old Army of the Tennessee! Sherman! destroyed and scattered? Impossible! impossible! But what can it all mean? Night of anxiety, mingled with hopes and fears.

August 29. — Council of war. To go or not to go, which? Inducements to remain — doubts and dangers ahead. Result of conference is, that all things considered, and reports true or false, we start for our lines this evening at dark. The writer had not much to give, but such as he had he placed at the disposal of Aunt Mary. The main gift was his silver watch. He took it from his pocket and passed it to Aunt Mary, and asked her to accept it with his sincere thanks for the aid and comfort she had furnished him, and for the deep interest she had taken in his welfare, as well as for the exhibition of loyalty to the cause represented by the uniform he wore. Aunt Mary seemed greatly surprised and embarrassed. She went through the usual *motions*, but was too black to blush. Sudden and unexpected. In the nobility of her nature, she said: "If you must give that away too, give it to brother Peyt." Peyt was all ears and eyes. In obedience to her request, the watch was handed over to Peyt. With both hands he accepted it. He appreciated the gift, but had long before proved more than his appreciation of the giver. The trusty timepiece had been a valuable companion, constantly imparting, by day and by night, much desired information; but the idea of leaving those tried and true friends with any thing in the way of personal property upon me, to which was not attached more significance than mere intrinsic value, seemed repulsive. in the extreme, and made the giving of the watch a real pleasure and not a sacrifice. "Peyt always did fancy that watch." In Aunt Mary's cabin the faithful had assembled to bid us good-bye and God-speed. We bade an affectionate farewell to all, and were soon rapidly marching eastward, *en route* to the Federal lines. Our plan is to round the Confederate right flank, which we learn is near Covington, Georgia, north-eastward, and perform a safe circle to the rear of the extreme Federal left, and to press eastward as long as danger threatened from the north. It was thought, as the Northern Georgia Railroad, extending eastward from Atlanta, had been, and probably continued, a "bone of contention," that we could reach that, and cautiously follow it toward Atlanta until "captured" by the Federal pickets or scouts. We cautiously proceeded, without uttering a word, a distance of between eight and nine miles, to a plantation of a "Mr. Gleaton," a wealthy Southern gentleman, where we had reason to believe much valuable information could be obtained from one of his negroes, named "Bill," who had recently returned from work on the entrenchments at Atlanta. We approached the cabin of a negro friend of Jim, and learned that "Bill" was on duty at his master's mansion, and could not be interviewed until after daylight. "Ordered"—a halt for the night; headquarters established in the woods, about one mile distant from the mansion; spot indicated and agreed upon; bedding furnished; sweet sleep until broad daylight of—

August 30.—We opened our eyes on a charming morning. Birds singing; squirrels sporting—dim light streaming through the foliage. Beautiful! Beautiful!

> "See how Aurora throws her fair
> Fresh-quilted colors through the air!"

No time wasted at the *toilet*. "Now, Jim, tell me,—

tell me about Mr. Gleaton and his family." Gathered that Mr. G. is wealthy land-owner — corpulent; built like Mr. Smith, but somewhat smaller — slaves call him a good master; feeds his slaves well; they are not obliged to steal to live well. Contrasted with Smith, to the latter's discredit; Gleaton generally kind and reasonable, but exceedingly cunning. He slyly approaches the hands at work in the field, and suddenly and unexpectedly appears in their midst. Appropriately dubbed, in consequence, "Old 'Poss." Strong Southern man — has sons in the Confederate army, or at least one — his son George is at home, *minus* a leg lost in the Confederate service. His son Thomas is too young for a man, and yet too old for a boy; he hunts squirrels with a small rifle. Both reported as given to intolerable boasting of individual ability to dispatch indefinite numbers of Yankees on sight! A daughter, too, — beautiful and accomplished. Descriptions interrupted by approaching footfalls — breathless attention — black faces; all right. Two of the field-hands, negresses, on their way to work, knowing of our presence, made us a pleasant morning call, and brought information that Bill was aware of our presence, and would bring us dinner. Interesting chat — surprised and delighted — continue their way, singing as they go. Noon brought the coveted Bill, with a warm, wholesome dinner for us. Introduction — information not important. "Niggers not 'lowed to know much, sar." Reports of Lybyer; all right when last heard from — at Freeman's, only three miles distant — determine to endeavor to overtake him to-night, and three go together. Night — thanks, and farewell. A short tramp over a path through fields and woods, and we are on the west bank of South River. A small scow, used by the negroes in crossing, and which they Frenchify by calling a "bateau," is in waiting for us; a short sail — the east bank — a mile-heat through fields and woods, and we reach the plantation called "Freeman's." "Tell me all about Freeman and family, Jim." Freeman, poor white — plantation belongs to Gleaton — Gleaton furnishes the hands, and Freeman superintends and works the place on shares; residence equidistant between South River on the west and "Honey Creek" on the east. The usual circling around behind the negro cabins. We are expected, and greeted with warm welcome and warm supper. Word "flew" over from Gleaton's by daylight that we might be expected to-night. We find another trusty friend in "Aunt Hannah," a great heavy, fat, jolly negress, "more'n half white." Happy to see us — delighted to aid us — full of kind wishes and congratulations — assisted Lybyer. "Where is he?" Started off last night — disappointment; his intentions or plan not ascertainable. Nothing from the armies — no news — silence Atlantaward! Our plan is to press rapidly forward — urgent invitations to remain declined, with sincere thanks. If Sherman is really going back, we certainly ought to follow him, even behind the enemy. Doubts harassing — we must press forward. Our objective — Conyers Station, on the Northern Georgia Railroad — only eight miles northward. Two slaves of Gleaton, working for Freeman, named "Jack" and "Near," tender their services as pilots — accepted as "advanced guards," thus enabling us to march rapidly. Thanks; full haversacks; farewell — on the march. Plan: "advanced guards," if captured, are "going to visit colored friends at Conyers." No "ear-marks" of intent to run away — in light plantation rigs, *sans* coats and shoes. Meantime we "act accordingly," to strike the railroad at Conyers and face Atlantaward. Eager for news; nearing Conyers; halt — listen — still as death! We can see the railroad-crossing. Glorious progress; welcome sight. Now, bidding our "advanced guards" farewell, we pass through the silent village street to the railroad, and turning our faces westward, walked steadily and rapidly until "driven from our position" by daylight of —

August 31. — Retreat to the thick woods; "headquarters" established — too near a fine residence; retreat to an uninviting swamp in the woods — broad daylight. No sound or indication of war — ominous silence; aggravating quiet. Voices — a reconnoissance by the writer disclosed a negro man and a white boy in an adjoining cornfield stripping leaves from corn-stalks (pulling fodder) — no reasonable opportunity to be neglected to ascertain the news. The writer returned to "headquarters," doffed his blue and donned the gray coat of Jim; circled around the field, and approached the workers from the opposite direction, hailing them to attract their attention. They both appeared much astounded, and curiously eyed the writer, with a cautious, inquiring gaze. "Good morning," said the writer, assuringly — they both simply nodded. "Any Yanks about here recently," was then inquired. "Yanks are falling back to Chattanooga," said the boy. (Did they notice the blood leave the writer's face?) "Then I am safe," said the writer, "to hunt our cavalry on the road, eh?" "Safe enough," said the negro — "Yanks done gone away." A white man was now nearing us. "Who's that?" inquired the writer. "That's my pa," said the boy. (Dreaded spectre; unwelcome visitor — old head.) Approach — a nod, a "how d'y." Old man quite inquisitive — uncomfortably curious — perplexing interrogatories — pressed for ready responses; upshot — Confederate, escaped from Yankee raiders, desirous of reaching Confederate forces. "What regiment?" "Twenty-fifth Georgia, Company K." His eyes cautiously scanned the *blue pants* of the Federal uniform. "Where did you gather those Yankee pants?" asked he. (Why is wit so slow? Why has ingenuity fled?) His eyes followed the little light-blue welt or cord down the outer seams. "Those, sir, — those sir, were kindly presented to me by a Yankee officer. You see, when

I escaped I ran through a creek, and my pants becoming wet and heavy, retarded me greatly, so I pulled them off, exchanging my pants for the chance to escape, but was afterwards overtaken by the blue devils and captured. Pity and decency moved a Yankee officer to lend me these — he had 'em strapped on rear of his saddle. Afterwards I again escaped, as you see." (Wonder how he'll take that?) "Well, well," said he, his face brightening to a credulous smile; "you did have quite a venture, sho' — but you needn't fear now — the Yankees are just scattering for Chattanooga, and Gen. Hood is right on 'em. They all are going back heap sight faster than they came." Ill-feigned delight. Will the darkness within eclipse the brightness without? Genuine gloom; false smiles — receding hope — momentary silence broken with: "Wont you come up to the house to dinner, sir? Some of our cavalry will be along directly." "I think I'd better seize the first opportunity to meet them, — I've left a little bundle in the woods, [blue coat and haversack] and thanking you for your kindness, I will get it and wait for them on the road; no time is to be lost. Good-day, sir;" and the writer left as he came, and circled around to tell Jim of the "glorious news." More concealed position in the woods selected — misgivings. Could the man have feigned credulity so well? Jim downhearted too; Sherman failed to take Atlanta — another head in the Washington basket. Old Army of the Tennessee will lose all its laurels in a retrograde movement — never had any experience in retreat — will surely be cut up. How can this report be true? how can it be possible? "Well, Jim, of one thing we may be certain: the campaign against Atlanta is not over. If Sherman has gone back, it is surely like the tide — only to come again afresh. Whipped? No, sir; you may be certain that the old army is not whipped without much more fuss and racket than we have heard. [Sherman had swung the army clear around the rebel left, in execution of the famous flank movement which won Atlanta.] "True, this silence gives credence to these reports — the army must have gone back, but that the campaign is not ended you may bet all you've got, Jim." Jim sadly shook his head — keen and bitter disappointment — consideration of the gloomy situation.

> "Disappointment's mist surrounds us,
> Dangers all around us bide."

In our front is — we know not what; in our vicinity we know of no one we can ask for a crumb of bread or of comfort, or to whom we can impart our secret. The immediately surrounding country has been pretty well "stripped" by both armies. Most of the negroes have fled to the Federal lines, or joined the column as it passed by. Those who remain may not be trustworthy, and if trustworthy, cannot be depended upon for rations — they can hardly get enough for themselves. In our haversacks we have rations for twenty-four hours — till to-morrow afternoon; what then? Under the circumstances, we cannot advance, — we cannot remain; the alternatives remaining are to retreat or surrender; the latter, never! until the — until — well, *never!* Determined upon safe retreat — twilight; dark; plan: to return to Conyers Station "by rail," and follow the road leading south to Freeman's. Since we must suspend "military movements" and patiently await developments and explanations, it is best to await them in comparative comfort and safety among friends. The march to Conyers — single file through its main street, Jim preceding — writer whistled, as best kind of deception. (A man feels at home when he whistles.) We travel in the middle of the road, as numerous ladies are parading the sidewalks bareheaded, in the cool air of the late evening, by twos and threes — *gentlemen* very scarce — families enjoying the cool evening chatting on piazzas — boys playing in the street. We pass all safely, and without a word spoken by us or to us; boldness disarms suspicion — the road leading south — leisure gait transformed to a brisk, rapid pace as we turn southward. Eight miles' rapid march and almost speechless transit, and shortly after midnight we rest our weary limbs at coveted Freeman's. Cautiously arousing Aunt Hannah — whispered explanation of return, and warm congratulations and welcome; we slept sweetly in quilts on her kitchen floor.

Awakened and retreated to the friendly woods at daybreak of —

September 1, — Where we remained awaiting developments all day, royally provided for by Aunt Hannah; dark; a conference of war — no artillery, no sounds of battle — no doubt something extraordinary has happened at the front. The negroes had always insisted that Freeman's folks were "Union," and now again insisted that the writer test their loyalty by disclosing his character and presence to them. The writer inquired: —

"What did they ever say to make you think so? They might have been just testing you."

"They often said they'd like mighty well to see a real Yankee."

"Ah, but any Confederate soldier might say the same."

"But one of the girls — Siss — says she's going to marry a Yankee."

"That was just by way of a joke."

"But I heerd old man Freeman say 'it was a great shame for our folks to try and break up the Union.'"

"That talk was all for *black* ears."

"Well, we's satisfied to have you try him. You'll find him 'Union,' strong!"

"Very well; I'll try him to-night, and we shall all see

whether he is Union or rebel. I don't think he would dare be Union if he wanted to."

Twilight — dark; plan of approach formed and announced. The writer wore a light, lavender-colored cape, which Aunt Mary had kindly and thoughtfully furnished, and it was dyed with sumach leaves, — as Aunt Mary expressed it, "de color ob night," — and served to nicely conceal the blue cloth, a row of glittering brass buttons, and shoulder-straps. "Pickets" were stationed on the road above and below the house, to cast a stone as the signal of the approach of cavalry, or other danger. These precautions taken, the writer stepped into the road, and silently passed to the front gate of the Freeman residence, which stood about ten feet back from the gate. A halt; listen; the customary hail — a young lady in "homespun" dress appeared at the window, and inquiringly peered toward the gate. She manifestly heard the hail, but, save by appearance, failed to respond. The writer then said, —

"I wish to see the man of the house, if you please."
Mr. Freeman then strolled slowly toward the gate. The writer opened conversation with —

"Who lives here, sir, please?"
"I do; my name is Freeman."
"How far is't to Conyers?"
"About eight mile, they say. Who are you?"

"Only a stray Confederate. Seen any of our cavalry lately?"

"Nary one since last week; don't know what's come o' them all of a sudden. Guess they've got enough of the Yankees."

"Why so, sir?"

"Well, it looks like it's becomin gmore and more up-hill work to fight 'em; we'd better give it up altogether."

"So I think, if there are many more *traitors* like you in the rear of our army."

"Well, that's the way I feel about it. It's only a clear waste of lives. They're too strong for us, sir. The government is bound to whip us, sooner or later. We all know we can't stand it much longer."

"Did you ever see a Yankee?"

"No, sir; but I wouldn't be afraid o' them; I never did a thing agin 'em in my life. I heerd tell so much about 'em, I would like right well to see one on 'em."

"Look at me! Do I look like a Confederate?"

"I reckon you do, sir; you're no Yankee, sir."

The writer stood in the flood of light which streamed from the window, threw back over his shoulders the little gray cape, exposing the blue uniform and glittering buttons and shoulder-straps. "What do you think now?"

Mr. F. started back with "What! Possible? A Yankee? You? I am your friend — you must not stand here on the road, in danger. Come in, sir; come in. My folks will be glad to see you." The family now gathered at the window, at the mention of the word "Yankee," which was excitedly repeated by them in whispers. As he was escorted into the room, a shawl was tacked up, as a substitute for a curtain, against the front window. "Our folks frequently pass on the road," said one. The little gray cape was doffed, and never was the wearer so proud of his blue uniform and straps as when these five pairs of admiring eyes scanned them. Steady gazing; curiosity mingled with admiration. "First Yankee ever seen." Cordial invitation to supper accepted, with thanks. An introduction to the members of Mr. Freeman's family disclosed the presence of Mrs. Freeman, Miss Downs, a buxom miss of eighteen summers (daughter of Mrs. Freeman by a former marriage), and called "Siss;" Milligan, her brother, aged about twelve years, stout, healthy, good-natured; Betsy and Nancy (daughters of Mr. Freeman by a former marriage), aged respectively seventeen and fifteen.

Mr. Freeman — Age about fifty-five; belongs to the Thirtieth Georgia Militia; owner of one slave woman, Sarah, and her child. One of the peculiarities of a peculiar system is exhibited in her case: her husband, called "Dock," is a free negro, hanging around the plantation, having purchased his own freedom, and living with his "wife," the personal property of Mr. Freeman. The child of this free negro is also the property of Mr. F., under the well-known law that the offspring of the *dam* is the property of the owner. Delightful contemplation! The law for *brutes* is the law for slaves — the title of the master superior to that of the father. Mr. F. not responsible for the law. Kind, good-natured gentleman; practical Christian, harmless, philosophical, matter-of-fact; not one

> "Who quarrels with his feed of hay
> Because it is not clover."

From their first meeting until the present time a valued, fast friend of the writer.

Mrs. Freeman — About fifty-five; though gentle, yet not dull — not talkative; rather *nonchalant* — quiet, earnest sympathy for the writer — motherly — cautious — dry wit.

Miss Tinzy Downs — Robust; picture of health; well-proportioned — eighteen — fair complexion, brown hair, blue eyes, pearly teeth — decided blonde — interesting expression and address — moves one to pity that poverty can limit culture — possesses the "handful of common sense" which "is worth more than a bushel of learning" — features interesting — Grecian.

Betsy Freeman — Quiet disposition; seventeen — enjoys a joke, but never manufactures or perpetrates one — *petite* blonde — fine hazel eyes — chestnut hair — always pleasant; cheerfully lends the writer her dresses, and laughs inordinately when they are donned to belie sex.

Nancy Freeman — Fifteen; full of life and frolic — talkative, vivacious, sparkling, interesting, sympathetic, sensible, mischievous.

Milligan Downs — Called "Mig;" twelve — thinks "lots" of his Yankee friend — proposes to go North with the writer, and "enlist in the Yankee army as drummer-boy" — cheerful, accommodating, inquisitive — never tires hearing about the Yankee army.

Jacob Freeman — Eldest son of Mr. F., and at present a private in the Confederate army, and on duty at Andersonville prison-pen.

Supper was announced in due time, and the writer partook heartily. He briefly related his experiences since within the rebel lines, and expressed his great delight to learn that *all* the whites were not rebels — delighted to find a few white faces that he could look into without fear and trembling. Great sympathy and interest were manifested in the writer's behalf. He now arose to depart, and expressed his gratitude for sympathy and encouragement. "But where are you going to-night?" inquired Mrs. F. "Oh, I shall find friends; the colored people always seem glad to provide for me some way." "But you have as good friends here; and you have no home, no friends, and will certainly be in danger outdoors; so stay with us all night, at least," pleaded Siss. "Better stay, I reckon," said Mr. F. "You can't have your cap," said Siss, as she clung to that article. Their invitations seemed stamped with sincerity, and the writer consented to be shown to the "spare room." (Soft bed, clean bedding, perfect trust, sweet slumber.) Habit of awakening and retreating at daybreak was not so strong as to disturb rest; and when the eyes opened, the sun was away up in the morning of —

September 2. — Dressing; toilet — almost forgotten luxury — morning greetings; mutual curiosity to meet by daylight — warm breakfast. "We are going to the field to work, pulling fodder; wouldn't you go along with us?" asked Mr. F. "Agreed; I used to work on a farm myself." "I have some negro boys who belong to my neighbor, and who visit there frequently; had we better tell them who you are? Would they *blab* it, think?" "Yes, tell them I'm a Yankee — accept my guaranty they'll not tell of it, if cautioned."

In the field — Freeman introduces my trusty friends and pilots, Jack and Near, to a "Yankee." (How naturally they feign surprise.) Perfect strangers. First favorable opportunity, Mr. F. received intimation that the writer had met the "boys" before — assertion substantiated by the boys. "I kind er thought so," said Mr. F., smiling. The writer put in a good day's work with the boys, Mr. F., and the three girls, who also acted as "field hands," pulling, binding, and stacking sheaves of fodder. The exercise by daylight was invigorating;

lunch at noon, warm supper at night. "How much sweeter a meal seems when we feel that we have well earned it," remarked the writer, while the laugh went round the table. About dusk, a rebel mail-carrier rode by the house, and, reining up at the gate, sadly made the astounding announcement, "The Yankees have taken Atlanta!" (Glory hallelujah! Yankee doodle! Get all the particulars. Thought they had been driven back! Where's Jim?) Nothing else — only the sad news, told with lengthened nasal twang, "The Yankees have taken Atlanta;" and the sad-eyed butternut calmly moves on. We unitedly rejoice. The blue-coats will be here to-morrow! Oh! too good to be true. But how was Atlanta taken? There's been no booming of cannon Atlantaward. There's a mystery about the whole business. Only, "it's taken!" Exultations; congratulations; conversation away into the night — retirement — sleep out of the question — rest feverish and fitful.

September 3. — Great excitement; work suspended. "The Yankees are coming!" "The Yankees are coming!" Through an abundance of precaution, the writer retired to a concealed spot in the woods, back of Freeman's, indistinctly commanding a view of the road, and all day long patiently watched for the blue-coats, as a cat watches for a mouse. Cannonading and musketry heard westward, in direction of Jonesboro, on the railroad. "Are the rebs retreating down the railroad?" "Push 'em back, 'Uncle Billy,' push 'em back; push 'em south of our 'position,' anyway." The day passes, and so do "great expectations." Not a soul passes on the road — everybody willing to stay at home; all seem tremblingly awaiting developments. Freemans extra proud of their guest, in whose presence they feel protection and favor from the "enemy." Getting quite aristocratic now — sleep under a roof.

Sunday, September 4. — Greater excitement. "Yankees certainly coming"— rebels demoralized, and falling back. Along the roads and lanes, and scattering through the woods and fields, straggle the defeated and disheartened Confederates; no longer an army — no longer an organization — disconnected and dispirited mob; devil-may-care airs — every man his own commanding officer; woods decidedly unsafe for blue cloth. The Freemans conceal the writer in their garret; comparatively good view of surrounding country from garret window — small volumes of blue smoke are curling gracefully skyward through the foliage, marking the numerous "camp-fires" of straggling soldiery. Siss turns spy for the Union cause; she hails the straggling, jaded soldiers in gray, and elicits valuable information. "What is the matter, sir?" asked she of an intelligent but tired and worn "gray-back." "Matter, ma'am! why the war is over! That's what ails us — we're going home." Another replied, "The Yankees are in Atlanta. We did our best to keep 'em out, but we are badly whipped; no use — nothin' but murder to put us before the Yankee guns." Butternut and gray only colored cloth on the road — patiently awaiting appearance of something *blue*. So the day and night pass.

September 5. — *Statu quo.* Anxiously and patiently awaiting the advent of blue cloth; still in the garret.

September 6. — Jim had been dispatched to Gleaton's and Smith's, to bear the news of our failure to reach our lines, and to gather information concerning the Federal advance, and to leave word with our friends to inform any genuine "blue-coats" of our situation. We were to meet by appointment at Gleaton's to-night; and accordingly, after dark, the writer, piloted by "Near," proceeded to the appointed place. The promise to return to Freeman's, in the event of failure to reach the Federals, was solemnly exacted and given. Farewell; a short march to South River — in the bateau — at Gleaton's — warm welcome. Jim not arrived; what can cause the delay? Anxiously waiting for Jim. "Wee sma' hours;" no arrival; pallet bed on floor of negro cabin for writer; grand fire on the hearth — slumber. Daybreak of —

September 7. — The retreat to the woods — no Jim — alone. The news is, "De Yankee *calvary's* advancing." Not a shot can be heard; difficult to reconcile so much war and so much "defeat" with so much silence — ideas of war all out of joint. Dead silence indicated "Sherman's defeat and retreat;" now "dead silence" indicates the advance of the Yankee "calvary." Verily the times are out of joint.

September 8. — Lonesome — anxious — watching. "Where's Jim?" Speculations wild and uncertain concerning his absence. "Has he been 'gathered' by cavalry?" Blue or gray? "Will he conduct the 'bluecoats' to me here?" Uncertainties, doubts, fears, hopes, and misgivings close the day.

September 9. — Solemn conference; conclude to wait for Jim one day longer only — in the woods at daylight. Suddenly voices were heard in the vicinity of the retreat, and a reconnoissance disclosed the approach of two young men with rifles and dog — squirrel-hunters. A closer view, and the writer recognized "Tommy Gleaton," whom he had previously secretly inspected at Freeman's. The writer was kept quite busy for some hours in evading the invaders of his retreat, and in endeavoring to keep his person to the leeward of the nostrils of the dog — chances of being observed at least seventy-five per cent greater while in motion. Shifting about tends to attract attention — extra cautious. On several occasions, felt compelled to move unceremoniously — series of rapid "flank-movements" and hasty "retreats" — finally driven to a pine grove, and eagerly penetrated it as a delightful retreat where squirrels are not found. The writer threw himself into a friendly gully, protected by sheltering pine boughs, and enjoyed rest. After the "skirmish" with the squirrels, the hunters started homeward on a path leading through the pines, which the writer had not observed, but which he now discovered ran within thirty feet of his retreat. Adown this path came the hunters, chatting cheerfully, the dog beside them — to attempt retreat would only insure instant discovery. A little closer nestling among the protecting boughs, a little flatter upon mother earth, and the dreaded trio passed unobservingly, and the critical moment was over. The dog alone seemed interested, snuffing the ground as he passed, and manifestly catching the scent of human footprints, but unable to distinguish between the blue and the gray. With great pleasure the writer observed their retreating forms lost to view in the thick pines. But in the shifting about, the writer was unable to retain any ideas of distance or direction, and became completely bewildered as to both; very effectually lost—he could only determine the points of the compass, but was utterly unable to even guess in which direction were friends and in which foes. While standing indulging in indefinite and unprofitable contemplation, eager to catch any sight or sound to indicate the direction of Gleaton's, the sounds of pattering hoofs were indistinctly heard. Nearer and nearer the sounds approached, until, through the thick boughs, the writer observed the mounted forms of six rebel cavalrymen — gray-coats — who passed on a road hardly twenty feet distant from him. A road so near? The sun was now nearly sunken behind the western horizon; not knowing the proper direction to take, the writer stood nonplussed, and listened. It was one of those calm, beautiful summer evenings, the death-like stillness only broken by feathered songsters of the forest, and the tinkling of distant bells in the pasture-fields; a flood of mellow, golden light streamed through the foliage, and all surroundings wore the aspect of gentle peace — but man. Hark! the deep, rich melody of a plantation-song floats upon the still evening air. "Field-hands returning from work; can it be possible they are Gleaton's, and that I am so completely turned around?" Listen to their plaintive wail — did you ever hear it? Mournful harmony — thrilling — would move a heart of adamant. Almost instinctively he followed the familiar, alluring voices, which conducted him safely to Gleaton's, and trusty friends. Word had been whispered among them that the Yankee was missing, the real cause instantly suspected, and the loud plantation-songs produced the very effect designed. Shrewd, sagacious allies; quick as a flash to comprehend a delicate situation without explanation. Faithful, trusty blacks. Shortly after dark, Jim quietly reappeared, and brought no important information about the armies. "Jim," said the writer, "you are well dubbed 'old dog;' where have you been smelling around?" "I'se been waitin' for the Yankees at Smith's; I couldn't get yere when we said, and I come now to get you." "What did I tell you about the Yankees, Jim — where's Atlanta now?" Aunt Mary had given the order to bring the writer to her "dis very night." "Dey's no 'scape — you must go," said Jim. Not unwilling to again greet Aunt Mary, and in the hope of increasing the chances of also greeting the blue-coats, the writer consented to go. Shortly before midnight we started, and were soon speeding across the fields. We arrive at Cotton River; a fire — voices — men. Blue or gray? We cautiously approach on hands and knees, screened by the shrubbery, until near enough to clearly observe a rebel picket-post. We quietly retreat, and complete the accustomed circle around them, keeping a sharp lookout for the sentry on the road, crossing the small river on a log, and rapidly proceed toward Smith's, boldly marching on the road. When about three miles east of Smith's, our ears suddenly caught the sounds of clattering hoofs; a halt — listen. Louder and nearer! "They're coming down the road!" Over the fence in a twinkle — concealment; now pass eastwardly a squadron of Confederate cavalry, at least one hundred strong; carbines — clanking sabres — talking in subdued tones. "Bye-bye, boys!" We were soon again on the march, and in due time arrived safely at Aunt Mary's. Our old friends are all up, patiently awaiting our arrival, and calmly sitting in the doors of their huts. They manifested much joy to again meet us; young and old must have a hearty "shake." Aunt Mary seemed very much affected; she embraced the writer affectionately, and declared, "I think jus' as much of you as if you was my own chile!" There was no "color line" before which could be halted the flow of genuine esteem and gratitude which the writer entertained toward true and tried black Aunt Mary.

"Skins may differ, but affection
Dwells in white and black the same."

The remainder of the morning was spent in slumber on a pallet bed in Aunt Mary's cabin-loft.

September 10. — The writer was informed that the woods were considered dangerous, and that he must remain in the loft all day; the march and excitement of the previous night, however, converts confinement into welcome rest. Confederate cavalrymen and stragglers on foot are wandering about from plantation to plantation, purchasing pigs, corn, chickens, potatoes, etc. They report that the "whole army is encamped at Jones-

boro" (on the railroad, only twelve miles eastwwrd).
"The Atlanta army fallen back!" The writer immediately determined that Smith's was no place for him.
He yearned for the other flank — the right of the Federals — as the rebels were manifestly being pressed eastward. At all events, he discovered that he was now *among*
the enemy, and either flank would be preferable to the
centre. The frequent visitations of "gray-backs" at
Smith's during the day made Aunt Mary's cabin uncomfortable "headquarters" for a "blue-coat." This agitation in Confederate military circles means something.
Determination to again attempt to reach our lines by
rounding the extreme flank of the Confederates as before.
There's no delusion this time — Sherman's *in* Atlanta!
Our cavalry raiders will certainly "hang about" the
rebel flanks — would prefer the other flank, but it's not
available. At dark we bid all a last, affectionate farewell, and rapidly march eight miles eastward, avoiding the
roads, and proceeding across the fields to Cotton River.
Here we find again the fire at the rebel picket-post on the
road, and from a safe distance cautiously inspect the gray
uniforms about the fire; maintaining, the while, most profound respect for the unseen sentry, whom we knew *ought*
to be standing in the dark on the road. We safely arrived
at Gleaton's — slept on pallet beds in a friendly negro
hut until daylight of —

September 11, — Which found us again in thick protecting foliage of the woods. After dark we were conducted to a neighboring plantation for a solicited conference with the writer, which had been requested by a negro slave and his wife, runaways, who desired to reach the Federal lines. They asked the writer, "Which way is best to go?"

"That's the very thing I can't tell for myself."

"Well, we'd like mighty well to go wid you."

"That will never do; two of us find travelling together very dangerous — four pair of feet would more than double the risk."

"We'll take all de risk, sar."

"But I'll not take any; your interest and ours requires separation; two can make quite enough noise. The writer observed the negro was armed with a carbine, and inquired, —

"Where did you get that rifle?"

"In de ribber yonder, off one o' you 'uns who was with Mr. Kilpatrick's raiders, and drowned in trying to ford de ribber."

"Let me see it." (Examines.) "A Yankee carbine, sure. Say, Sam, better give me this carbine; it belongs to the Yankees, anyhow. I'll make good use of it, if you'll give it to me; beside, it would go pretty hard with you to be caught by the rebs, armed."

"I done thought o' that befo'—guess you'd better take it along."

"Thank you, Sam (negroes all 'Sams'); thank you."

"Here's a few cartridges for 't—take 'em along."

"Thank you—thank you."

"An' here's a few caps for 't, too."

"Thank you."

The writer pressed the steel clasp beneath the stock, the breech slid downward, and the handy little breech-loading Federal carbine was soon loaded and capped—ready for action. Glorious! "I feel as strong as a whole regiment. No longer required, under any and all circumstances to play the 'sneak;' can assume the offensive now, if absolutely required—arms and ammunition;" keen realization of difference in feeling between being armed and unarmed. Reminded of slight difference humorously alleged to exist between Confederate and Democrat, viz., " Confederate, armed Democrat; Democrat, unarmed Confederate." The reflection forced that if the "slight difference" extends beyond mere sentiment or opinion, it immediately enlarges to one of magnitude. Returned to Gleaton's an armed Yankee—glowing expressions of over-confidence in the negroes of the Yankee's ability to use the weapon if required. Slumbered sweetly on a pallet on the cabin floor, my trusty carbine my "bedfellow." Between two and three o'clock in the morning of—

September 12, — We were gently aroused by "Near," one of Freeman's field-hands, who stated that the Freemans, especially Siss, had dispatched him for the writer, with instructions "not to return without him." "They have some important news, probably." The writer willingly obeyed the unseasonable summons, and in a few moments was on the march toward Freeman's, accompanied by the faithful messenger, leaving Jim to await his return to Gleaton's. The bateau was missing from the river-bank; but without stopping to investigate the cause, the writer and his guide hastily stripped off their clothing, carrying it on their heads while they forded the river, over waist-deep; then hastily dressing, and rapidly marching, safely reaching their destination about sunrise. The usual precaution developed that "Grandpa" (Mrs. Freeman's father) was up on a visit from Oak Hill, Georgia (six miles southward), and it was deemed wise to withhold our secret from him. Accordingly, Near was dispatched to report to Freeman's the presence of the writer, and returned to the woods with "Dere's no news in partic'lar; Siss say she want to see you, dat's all." "She has news she will not tell Near," thought the writer. Patiently waiting in the woods, with growing confidence in my loaded companion-piece; as usual, my selected position commands all the approaches to the house. Toward evening, Siss appeared at the rear window of the kitchen building, situated some distance in rear of the residence, and peered inquiringly into the woods. A form in blue disclosed its presence, and she beckoned its approach; cheerful obedience — greetings and congratulations. The young lady explained: "The old gentleman at the house is my grandpap; but he will go home soon, perhaps to-night, then we want you to come to the house. He is old, and if he knew a Yankee was about, he'd be scared to death."

"Why did you send for me, Siss; have you any news about our troops?"

"Not a word; I just thought you'd be safer here than anywhere else. Be sure and come to this window after dark; I'll have a nice supper for you."

"How can I ever repay you for your kindness?"

"Never mind that — you're friendless now."

"Friendless! then who are you?"

"Be sure and come early to supper, while it's hot; so good-bye till supper time;" and the pleasant face faded from the window like a vision. The writer cautiously retired to the woods, but saw nought but the pleasant face at the window; heard nought but a cheerful, sympathetic voice; merry birds warbled their evening songs, and squirrels vigorously chattered as if chiding his silence and lack of attention, but they interrupted not his thoughts. "Fair complexion, intelligent features, sparkling blue eyes, sweet voice, pearly teeth, fine figure; manifests great interest; large heart; rich brown hair —

and all growing more and more beautiful every moment! Why is this thus?" The voices of the night reminded him of the approach of darkness, which now steals, unobserved, over earth and sky. A hasty repairing to the appointed window; Siss was in waiting, and proudly passes out a delicious supper, which was fully appreciated and speedily appropriated. Said she: "Mr. Freeman's son 'Jake' is just up from the Confederate army, from Andersonville, where he is stationed on guard duty; but we've talked it all over, and decided that you're not going to sleep in the woods nor any cabin to-night. Grandpap and Jake both will stay all night, but we've made room for you too; so in about two hours, when every thing is quiet, please come to the house to sleep." Siss's programme was executed, and the writer slept soundly, separated by a thin board partition from the Confederate soldier, to whom it was thought not best to impart the "family secret."

September 13. — The writer was the first of the three visitors up, and was soon after in his retreat in the woods. By appointment, Milligan and the writer retreated deep into the forest together, and there tested the accuracy of the "Yankee carbine," shooting several times at a paper mark, at about four hundred yards distance; result entirely satisfactory. We returned about noon, and were informed that both "grandpa" and

"Jake" had departed — one for Oak Hill, the other for Andersonville. In our absence, the girls had studied an ingenious plan by which acquaintance with the writer was to be maintained by daylight as well as by night; he was to be disguised as a young lady. After a "clean shave," the writer was directed to don one of Betsy's calico dresses and a sun-bonnet. Done — splendid fit! "I'm to pass for Betsy, and poor Betsy's to stay at home while the rest of us raid for muscadines and grapes." Thus does the ingenuity of the girls anticipate undue curiosity of the neighbors, and also render their stranger-friend cavalry-proof. "Agreed; I'm Betsy." We venture forth on the road, accompanied by the little dog "Trip," and each carrying a basket; it seems so queer, so irregular, to be moving during daylight. A short distance from the house we met two strange horsemen, who gracefully lifted their hats and smiled pleasantly as the "three Freeman girls" passed. We pass "Honey Creek," finally reach the vines, gather the delicious fruit, and safely return with filled baskets; a success.

September 14. — Visitors' day; caught in the house early this morning — *i.e.*, unable to get out without great danger of being detected by old Mr. Gleaton, the proprietor of the plantation; on shares with Freeman. "Came over on a tour of inspection," he said, as he reined up his charger at the gate, before the writer awoke; "early bird." Yards, cabins, and work in the fields were scrutinized in turn, from a commanding position in the saddle. The writer obtained not a very satisfactory view of the "Old 'Poss," and was exceedingly cautious, after the frequent warnings by the negroes of the sly nature of the old gentleman. Shortly after noon he departed, and we all breathed freer. Before advantage of his absence could be taken, however, a Confederate soldier called; seated himself in the front-room, and seemed disposed to make himself very much at home, and actually tried to be funny. Siss was "detailed" by the writer to obtain any information she could from him, and the writer inspected him through a door slightly open at his back. He knew little more than we; was disposed to prolong his stay; tired everybody out; pointed hints were ineffectual; manifestly, as Siss said, waiting for an invitation to supper. Receiving no encouragement in that direction, he finally arose, stretched himself, and rode off supperless. No sooner had he gone than "Old 'Poss" returned, and remained all night, sleeping in a room adjoining that of the writer. His suspicious return caused some suspicion that he was curious about something. "Has he received a hint of our secret?" "Did he observe any thing which excited his curiosity?" Howbeit, he gained no further information by "roosting" away from his home.

September 15 and 16. — At Freeman's; dodging "neighbors" and rebel cavalry. Passing to and fro on the road are soldiers in gray, and also many refugees fleeing from the Yankees. We put on a bold front, however, and kept the family supplied with grapes and muscadines. The novelty of the writer's apparel — Betsy's dress — furnished not only healthy diversion for himself, but almost boundless amusement for the family. But the transition from frivolity to discretion was instant upon the approach of danger, or occurring circumstances which rendered good acting necessary; at other times, or when "off guard," much merriment was created by the writer's imitations, in costume, of many of Betsy's peculiarities.

September 17. — The new programme is for the writer to wear one of Betsy's dresses during the whole day. "If it be a good deception in emergencies, it cannot be bad in general; *ergo*, wear it. Plan adopted. Mr. Freeman seriously inquired of the writer, "But, George," (they had all learned to call the writer by his first name) "if our folks should happen to catch you in disguise, wouldn't they take you and hang you for a spy?" "No, not according to any laws of war; of course not. I didn't come, but was *forced* into their lines by them; but, of course, there's no telling what might be done. It might be hard for me to furnish other evidence than my own word that I am not a spy; even you don't *know* what I am. The only evidence on me is my diary; it's hard to tell how they'd construe that. However, such speculations will impress us with the importance of not being caught. I'll keep my uniform on, and take my chances in calico over it; I will not be disguised for any of the purposes of a spy." Free as a bird! Unbodied joy! Freedom of the yard, house, porch, and road by daylight; a new creature; a new life; relieved of the necessity of the constant strain produced by forced caution and concealment. The negroes seem wild with merriment! "Errand-girl" between whites and blacks. No Confederate, no Yankee — simple *non-combatant*.

September 18. — No sounds of war! "Where's Jim?" "What's the news? Why no report from the front? Has 'Uncle Billy' pushed 'em south of Smith's yet?" The writer undertook to obtain answers to these inquiries, especially the latter, in person; and at dark made an announcement to that effect, bade a reluctant good-bye, and carrying carbine and ammunition, proceeded on the usual route to Gleaton's with Jack, paddling across the river, tramping through the fields, and in due time was again welcomed at Gleaton's, and slept soundly in a friendly cabin.

September 19. — Usual march at daybreak for the woods. In straggling through the heart of the lonely woods for exercise, the writer suddenly came to a deserted, isolated, and partially dilapidated cabin, thickly surrounded by foliage; no signs of occupancy; a cautious approach, an entry, an investigation; suspicious appearance of the floor — boards loose; they readily yielded — up, and underneath lies concealed a small trunk. It is raining hard, and consequently safe to further investigate; tempting curiosity. The trunk is pulled out; fortunately a key is in possession which unlocks it, and justifies suspicions. The contents are noted: One gray Confederate uniform, a number of United States government shirts, a United States government sabre, a sample of Yankee cartridges, an assortment of fine new citizens' clothing, and a Yankee relic in the shape of a small edition of the New Testament. All "contraband of war," and fairly recaptured. The "government property" was concealed in a hollow tree near the cabin, where it may yet remain; the other property was left in the trunk. The "owner," upon exhibiting proper evidences of his title to the contraband articles, can now ascertain their exact location. The "Yankee relic" Testament was converted into a "Confederate relic," and is now in possession of the writer as such; it will be cheerfully surrendered upon request of the possessor of a superior title. Suddenly the thought occurred, "The negroes will be at once suspected, and perhaps punished." A happy thought — "show your hand" —

writing; negroes can't write like that! A fly-leaf is torn from the Testament; a pencil from the trunk writes substantially these words: —

"To the depositor of the contraband of war missing from this trunk: We are but a few Federals who have recaptured this government property, while on a short scout. The main army will probably pass in this vicinity shortly, when a proper account may be demanded; until then, farewell. FEDERAL SCOUTS."

"There," thought the writer, "that will turn suspicion from my colored friends, anyway." The note was left on the trunk, the trunk on the floor, and the weeds trodden down and shrubbery broken, to strengthen credulity. The writer mused, "These were no doubt concealed in anticipation of the Federal advance." For the first time, through this volume, those who already know a part of the facts may now also know the secret of them.

September 20. — In the cabins last night, and the trunk experience was related to tickled negroes; ownership of the trunk a mystery. In the woods at daybreak; a rainy, disagreeable day. "Headquarters" in a large, hollow tree; young negro boy, "Tommy," seemed delighted with the honor of bringing the writer a fine warm dinner; the writer was equally delighted to receive it. At night an opportunity was presented to obtain a closer view of the family of Mr. Gleaton, of whom the writer had recently heard so much highly "colored," harmless gossip. Through the crotch of a peach-tree he calmly viewed them at supper — a few feet away; every indication of intelligence and refinement; beautiful young lady. Before midnight, Jack arrived from Freeman's, under orders from "Siss," to ascertain what had become of the writer — if he had reached the Federal lines, and if not, to find him, "and not return without him." The writer willingly followed Jack back again to Freeman's, reaching there at daybreak of —

September 21. — Report received that Confederate soldiers are continually passing on the road, and officers frequently enter the house to make inquiries and indulge in idle chat. The residence deemed unsafe for "blue cloth," or for any presence which might excite curiosity. A comfortable pallet on the floor of Aunt Hannah's kitchen nicely meets the emergency.

September 22. — Confederate soldiers passing all day; many visit the negro quarters to purchase or confiscate chickens. Deep woods considered the only safe retreat for a straggler in blue.

September 23. — Extraordinary commotion, — rebel troops, cavalry and infantry, passing northwardly! Soldiers in gray overrun the plantation. Deep ravine, four hundred yards to the rear of the cabins, is the safe position to which the "blue" falls back. Inquiries made by Siss of some of the officers develop that the troops are ignorant of their destination. "Is it a counter flank-movement against Atlanta?" Whatever it means, it seems certain the campaign is not yet ended; the broken columns are slipping from Sherman's front, and passing to his flank and rear. Oh for a balloon to carry this news to our lines!

September 24. — "Confeds. all passed," they say; considered "safe to come in;" welcome; watching — waiting — speculating — guessing — drooping — dreaming. Prospects fast fading; demoralization — desperation!

Sunday, September 25. — Still in the "slough of despond." As the writer sat gloomily brooding over fading prospects, with face buried in his hands, he suddenly felt a stream of cool water course down his spinal column, and heard the sweet voice of Siss saying, "George, wake up! You must be jolly and cheerful; I'm not going to let you mourn about yere." After the first shock of the irregular baptism had passed, the cool joke, perpetrated in the spirit of mischief, simply elicited a ghastly smile on the writer's countenance; but a sly repetition, accompanied by a roguish laugh, proved too much for good nature; and as the merry torturer approached the third time, remarking, "This is your bathing day, anyway," the contents of a concealed glass of water suddenly splashed in her roguish face, and before she could recover from the shock, the contents of the glass intended for the writer also bathed her chestnut tresses. "There," said he, "guess you've got enough, now," and returned to his seat and indulgence in reverie. Quick as a flash, the entire contents of a large water-bucket fell upon his head and over his person, soaking his clothing completely through. "That'll wake you up," said the perpetrator of the deed, as she beat a swift retreat, followed by her completely drenched opponent, who seized a filled water-pitcher *en route*, and emptied its contents over her retreating person. "There," said he, "now folks 'll think we're Baptists." There was a cessation of hostilities; retirement, dry clothes, and a calm after the "showers." "The Yankees won't stand every thing, you see," said Mrs. F. to Siss, reprovingly, while the others seemed to enjoy our mutual discomfort.

September 26, 27, and 28. — Still at Freeman's, in female attire; simple repetition of scenes and incidents already described as occurring at Freeman's. Confederate stragglers daily passing northward, evidently to join their commands. "What does this rush on Sherman's left flank mean?"

September 29. — To-night Jim put in an appearance again. His colored friends had contributed and presented to him eighteen dollars in Confederate scrip, to assist us in our extreme poverty. Unable to use it otherwise, it was presented to Mr. Freeman by the writer. Jim has just come from Aunt Mary's, and brings information of rumors of "blue-coats," and that the Confederates "are all done gone," and suggesting that we again attempt that end of our "line of communication." We act on the suggestion; and after nine miles' march, during which we discovered and circled around the picket-post, still maintained at Cotton River, we again receive a cordial welcome from dusky friends at Aunt Mary's. After the usual fine supper, Jim repaired to a neighboring plantation for information, while the writer was nicely provided with a pallet in the old cabin-loft. Nothing definite, or satisfactory, or consoling concerning the armies, only "the Yankees are still in Atlanta." "What does Mr. Smith say now about the Yankees taking Atlanta?" inquired the writer of Aunt Mary. "He's mighty sober — don't say any thing," was the reply.

September 30. — Jim and the writer in the familiar bower-retreat in the woods; council of war; no Yankees — no encouragement — no inducements — hopeless. Determination to make a last, desperate effort to reach the Federal lines. We have waited long enough for our friends in blue to come to us; now we must go to them, or — or something worse! Dark; warm supper; announcement of intentions — last farewells. Many negroes offer services and company to our lines; kindly declined, with satisfactory explanations and thanks; final departure, amid exclamations of "God bless you!" "De Lord be wid you!" The night was fearfully dark; dark, heavy clouds stretched across the heavens, and all nature seemed hushed with fear at the approach of the threatening storm. Neither trees, nor roads, nor fences could be distinguished through the darkness of the night. Cotton River crossed, but impossible to keep the path through the woods beyond it. After slow and weary progress, and frequent contacts and stumblings, we safely reached "Gleaton's." We had just entered a friendly cabin, when the threatening storm burst forth with unusual fury — deluge of water. The rain-drops pattering against the exterior of the protecting cabin lulled the writer to sleep upon the comfortable pallet provided for him, his carbine — constant companion and bedfellow — at his side.

October 1. — Daybreak found us in the woods, the hollow old poplar furnishing ample protection from the rain. Bill acted very acceptably as our commissary during the day. No news yet. We announced to our friends our purpose to make a last desperate effort to reach our lines. At night, by arrangement, there was a "farewell" assembling of our colored friends; we held a short conference, returned our heartfelt thanks (all we had) for kindness and favors; bade all friends at Gleaton's a last good-bye, and after the usual effort, and marching through the rain, reached Freeman's about midnight. Jim repaired to the cabins; the writer was kindly admitted to the residence by Mrs. F., who discreetly tacked shawls to the windows, kindled a rousing fire on the hearth, and enabled the writer to dry his clothes; after which he was kindly shown to bed, and slept sweetly until late in the morning of —

October 2. — He was awakened by a gentle tapping on the door, and the familiar voice of Siss informing him that breakfast awaited him. Plantation-hands are now busy gathering "syrup-corn," the product of which is called "these syrup" and "them molasses." "George, try some of these yere syrup," said Mrs. Freeman to the puzzled writer. Suppressed smile. Aggravation for Mig. to blurt out, "Please pass them molasses." Not able to longer restrain pent-up curiosity, and seeking the most polite form of relief, the writer asked Mig, "Mig, why do you call the molasses 'them?'" "That's what we all call 'em," quickly responded Mrs. F. The explanation barred further inquiry, and of course was ac-

cepted as satisfactory. After breakfast there was a call for
the writer. Something extraordinary! One of the negroes
excitedly told him there was a Yankee in the woods (indicating the spot) who claimed to know Lieut. Bailey, of
Gen. M. L. Smith's staff, and requested to see him; but
that he "wore a Confederate uniform." How now —
a ruse, a trick? A hasty glance at the Freemans thoroughly convinced the writer of their innocence. Could
they do it? Curse the thought! Whatever it may mean,
whoever it may be, I'll see him; but I shall be armed.

"You may say to him that I'll see him presently in the
woods where he is.". The negro departed with the message. The writer took his loaded carbine, and to guard
against possibilities, circled away around the indicated
concealment, and cautiously approached the spot from
the direction opposite to that of the house. "There he
is, anxiously peering toward the house — his back toward
the writer." Near by him sat two negro women and
some negro children (runaways), who accompanied him.
The writer still cautiously approached unobserved to
within a few yards of them and halted, and cautiously
scanned the gray rebel uniform — object of suspicion,
though stuffed with straw. He's unarmed; wears gray
whiskers. All eyes strained toward the house, waiting for
a friend. "Hello!" hailed the writer. All eyes turned
instantly, and gazed inquiringly at the armed Yankee in
blue. The one in Confederate gray arose and exclaimed,

"Why, Lieutenant, how d'ye do?" He recognized the writer at once; expressed great delight to again look upon a Federal uniform; related how he had escaped from the "pen" at Andersonville; said he was a sergeant in the Fifty-third Ohio Infantry, and that his negro companions were runaways, "crazy to reach the Federal lines." The writer did not remember the sergeant, but placed implicit confidence in his story. At night, through the influence of the writer, the sergeant was invited to supper at Freeman's, and we all chatted pleasantly with him until word came that his dusky friends were awaiting him in the road, when he bade us good-bye, with many thanks and with well-filled haversack. A proposition for the writer to join them met with a piteous protest from Jim, and fierce opposition from the Freemans; besides, the sergeant agreed that on such expeditions "the fewer the better." Mutual messages were given for delivery within the Federal lines. The writer never heard of the sergeant afterward.

October 3. — The road is almost blocked to-day with the wagons of fleeing refugees, who tell tales of woe, and endeavor to induce a general flight before the advancing enemy. Siss gathers the information from them that Sherman and Hood are "playing chess" in rear of Atlanta, but that Yankee infantry had driven the Confederates from Flat Shoals (a point nearly midway between Freeman's and Atlanta). Mr. Gleaton is hurriedly repairing his wagons, preparatory to joining the general flight of refugees. His negroes are also arranging to retreat — the other way. Freeman's family, like all the "poor white trash," is to be cruelly left to the mercy of the hideous foe.

October 4. — A clear, mild, beautiful day. Siss sagely remarked, "It isn't necessary for us to keep in-doors just because there's so many frightened fools outside." Accordingly, clad in Betsy's dress and protected by a projecting sun-bonnet, Siss, Nancy, and the writer repeated the experiment of travelling the road for muscadines and grapes. *En route* to the vines we were met by a corpulent gent, mounted, and clad in butternut. "A neighbor," whispered Siss, as he approached us. He gallantly raised his hat and smiled pleasantly as he passed us, manifestly mistaking the writer for Betsy. "What if he stops at the house, and sees Betsy?" asked the writer. "He may stop at the house," said Siss, "but he can't see Betsy — ma's arranged all that." (Sagacious old lady.) "He's an old rebel for you — bitter as gall." We reached the vines, crossing Honey Creek on a log, and soon gathered our baskets full. The writer cut a very ridiculous figure in attempting to climb the trees over which the vines ran, to shake off the fruit; but his awkwardness and accidents attributable to surplus dry-goods only created the more merriment for the party. When returning, we were met on the road by Mig, who had been sent to warn us that "Tommy Gleaton" was at the house, ostensibly for the purpose of assisting Mr. F. work, but whose real object doubtless was to hunt some negroes who had recently run away from his father. The woods, consequently, were deemed unsafe. Upon observing our approach, Mrs. Freeman, under some pretence, induced "Tommy" to accompany her to the kitchen-building, across the yard, while the writer, with the other girls, safely entered the residence and protection.

October 5. — Open question: "What is Tommy's secret mission?" (He innocently slept under the same roof with the writer last night.) Extra caution was based upon our inability to solve the question. "Headquarters" to-day — stretched on a pallet spread under the bed of the "spare room." While the young object of suspicion was in the field with Mr. F., the writer inspected his little squirrel-rifle he had left in the house; handy little piece — nicely finished — light; throws round ball; indications of being much used; no match for my carbine; like most rifles — dependent for efficiency on the *stuff* behind it. During the evening, as this proprietor's son sat chatting before the grand hearth-fire in the dining-room, the writer embraced the opportunity of a closer inspection of his person, from without, through an open rear-door— Siss kindly acting as a screen. Tall, slim figure; smooth, beardless face; say, about nineteen; long legs; great feet — out of all manner of proportion; wears the great luxury of boots; mystery— how he can "navigate" in bad weather, encumbered with such *valises;* sits in the house with his soft hat on (manners); "sweet" on the girls; "snubbed twenty times a day;" forced to do most of his talking to the "old lady;" good shot on squirrels — frequently shoots them through the head. Desperately hates any thing *blue;* "can vanquish five Yankees." Boasting boy! (Like wine, "Tommy" has doubtless improved with age.) Is to stay again all night to-night; suspicions again aroused. The writer proposes to sleep in one of the negro cabins. "No." In the woods, then? "No." In the house? "Yes." But if Tommy should have confederates or friends outside, to enter at midnight? Ingenuity of the girls never "at sea." "You shall sleep with us." After the writer had partially recovered from the sudden shock produced by this announcement, he, in bewilderment, inquired of them, "What! With you?" (Profuse blushes at his stupidity, illy concealed by subdued laughter.) "Yes, on a pallet in our room; you'll be safe there, for no gentlemen would attempt to intrude into the privacy and bed-chamber of young ladies, for any purpose." The writer's attempt at relief by a proposition to retreat to Gleaton's or Aunt Mary's, met with an emphatic "no such thing." By the unanimous approval and assistance of the family, the writer's natural modesty was overcome, and he cheerfully "accepted the situation;" and, at the proper time, was ensconced in the safe and novel retreat, in half-undress uniform resting securely on the pallet in one corner of the room while the three girls slumbered in their accustomed bed in the other corner. There were a few whispered remarks made by the trio of amused girls, about the "flank movement" made on suspicion; a whispered defiance; suppressed laughter; a calm, motherly injunction from Mrs. F., in the adjoining chamber, to "be quiet, girls;" suppressed tittering, which soon subsided, and all became quiet — lulled in the soothing arms of Morpheus.

October 6.— Last evening was the time appointed by the writer *positively* to start for the Federal lines with Jim, but he did not appear, and his absence is the cause of no little apprehension. Now muse we on this theory: "Jim has been caught, threatened, questioned, and compelled to account for his presence in the neighborhood, and under promise of good treatment, delivered his secret. Young Gleaton is but a spy, or entering wedge, to effect a 'lodgement' in the Yankee's 'headquarters,' whom he expected to 'run against' last evening; it being the appointed time to start with captured Jim. He had ample assistance, no doubt, near at hand, and perhaps rebel soldiers, who were to 'move forward' at a given signal, and all make neighborhood heroes of themselves by capturing a live, armed Yankee." "Believe it? Of course not; but don't it look as if it might be so?" inquired the writer of Siss, who had patiently listened, with credulous glances, but who promptly replied, with flashing eyes, which never looked so beautiful before, "They couldn't take you while I lived — never!"

"But they would brush you away like a cobweb. Please help me to retain the little 'ounce of prevention,' and you'll not be troubled, in desperation, to attempt a 'cure.'" The writer assured his friends that he fully realized that he was armed, determined, and desperate as a "rat in a corner," and that if any persons succeeded in reaping "honors" at his expense, it would be for him to see that they well earned them. His often-announced plan was to always retreat as far as possible, and only to fight when absolutely unavoidable. But whether in retreat or fight, so long as he possessed arms he never intended to surrender. The utmost caution is to be exercised until Jim's failure to appear last evening, according to programme, be fully accounted for, and it be determined whether his absence is in any way connected with the other's presence. About noon we experienced a genuine sensation: "The Yankees are coming — the Yankees are here!" Tommy Gleaton, who was in the house at the time, will remember well how he unceremoniously "skedaddled" to the woods, much to the amusement of the family and the writer, who was excitedly summoned from his concealment to meet the blue-coats. He glanced up the road, and sure enough, there they came — the blue-coats! A nearer approach developed that they were unarmed. "Prisoners!" flashed across his mind; caution enjoined; they near — they pass the house — twenty, at least; four mounted Confederates follow behind them. Subdued feeling of indignation that four can guard twenty through lonely marches on unfrequented roads — twenty healthy, stout, coffee-drinking blue-coats meekly submitting to the guardianship of four sleepy-looking "grays." Raining hard — wet, muddy, slippery — poor fellows! It was dark before Tommy discovered his mistake, and no one took interest enough to search for him in the woods and rain. He returned with clothing wet through, and his attention was occupied for a considerable length of time in drying them. Pursuant to previous arrangement, he, with two of his young friends, after supper, departed with dogs, rifles, and torches, on a "coon-hunt." Great suspicion that they are playing "patrollers," and hunting two-legged coons. Their departure afforded the family and writer great relief, and all misgivings vanished as the welcome announcement was made that Jim, the renegade, had put in an appearance, equipped and ready for a march. The writer sought him, and after numerous lame excuses for absence, he announced himself ready to "move on our lines" to-night. Agreed. The writer announced this intention to the family, all of whom rather looked upon the undertaking as extremely hazardous; but he was impatient, and determined to wait upon uncertainties no longer. First he bade his colored friends a last farewell, then final preparations were made for departure. Three locks of hair; two cloth haversacks made by Siss, and well filled — one with wheat biscuits and roasted pork, the other containing a change of underclothing provided by herself — the carbine, and additional ammunition for the same, manufactured by appropriating and placing the powder from rebel cartridges behind Union bullets. The cartridges taken by the negro runaway from the cartridge-box of the Union cavalryman drowned during Kilpatrick's raid had been, of course, wet, and the powder had "caked," and was unreliable; but brown paper, Confederate powder, linen thread, and combined ingenuity soon put dry Confederate powder in "position" to speed Union bullets through a Yankee carbine. Military maps of the country printed on linen cloth, pocket-compass, canteen, diary, and small pencil comprised the "baggage" of the writer (most of which he now possesses as relics of the trip). The writer then prepared and handed to Mr. Freeman written acknowledgments of his loyalty and kindness, commending his family to the favorable consideration of all Federal officers and soldiers. The announcement that Jim was "waiting at the gate," created a flutter, and plainly disclosed the fact that pent-up feelings could not be concealed much longer. The little gray cape was hurriedly adjusted, the trusty loaded carbine seized, a shower of thanks tendered, a last "farewell" uttered, — a sudden start for the open door, and the threatened storm burst forth. Siss, without uttering a word, suddenly threw her arms about the writer's neck and sobbed aloud. Then the "floods" came, and the whole circle wept. What! moisture on the cheeks of a soldier deemed fit for desperate undertakings? Brush it away, and prove superior to circumstances before which *women* quail. The poor girl's explanation of her conduct was: "I have a gloomy presentiment that danger and harm await you, and that you will never see your home and friends again. Do not go; stay where we know you are safe — wait for your folks to come here." The others added their advice to wait in safety. The writer replied that it was beyond him to express his gratitude for their kindness and sympathy, and the interest they took in him, but reminded them that since July 22d he had been striving to reach the Federal lines; that he had now waited for our cavalry more than a month, and prospects of their coming seem lessening; that he now deemed it his duty to make this effort, dangerous as it might seem; but that his mind was made up, and he

felt almost strong enough to force his way to his lines
if necessary; and, besides this, his friends in the army
and at home could not have the faintest idea of his whereabouts. "Now, consider all these things, and feel with
me that I ought to go." The argument met the only
response of deep, expressive sobs. There was a moment
of silent sadness, and the writer stepped out upon the
porch, urging, "Now bid me a cheerful, last good-bye."
The family followed to the porch; each one save Mr. F.
bestowed a parting kiss. Mrs. F. said "Good-bye,
George; I feel as sad as though I was parting from my
own son." The sobbing young ladies and Mig could
only mutter "Good-bye."

> "You sadly press the hands of those
> Who thus in love caress you,
> And soul responsive beats to soul
> In breathing out, 'God bless you.'"

But resolution, firmness, courage, must supplant tenderer feelings now. I must

> "Hide this feeling at the heart,
> And bid a careless, light good-bye."

The writer was now at the gate with his companion,
Jim. Mr. Freeman accompanied the writer a few yards
down the road, tightly clasping one of his hands in his
own, expressing hopes of success, and many thanks for
the poor returns for generosity and sympathy of his family. He assured him that his family could never forget
him, and would always look back with intense interest

and pleasure to the days he had spent at his house; now a long, strong, earnest "shake," and Mr. F. returned. The writer paused an instant, looked back gratefully at the receding light in the window, and the loud sobbings of grief-stricken Siss were the last sounds he heard at Freeman's. With an instinctive dread, we penetrated the gloom of the night, continually casting longing glances behind at the friendly light in the window, growing fainter and fainter, until lost to our view. The dark curtain of night falls behind us on an immediate past of grateful and pleasant memories, and there's a dark one before us about to rise on an immediate future of — we know not what. We now marched rapidly northward, speechless. Thoughts driven to the front rush to the rear. Experiences bearing the stamp of romance: romantic introduction; extended protection; genuine sympathy; undissembled interest; unlooked-for kindness; willing sacrifices; poor, but true to the old flag. Thoughts flashing in vivid recall of chief incidents of the stay at Freeman's. Ne'er did one leave "home" with more regret; ne'er was one followed by purer sympathy. That evil *presentiment*. Don't believe in 'em? Nor I; but still haunted by that earnest plea to heed the solemn warning of another. A hasty summing-up results in entertaining sincere regrets at parting from friends and safety, to face unknown dangers. However, a motion to reconsider was immediately ruled out of order.

"To the front! to the front we speed."

Six miles from Freeman's, we reach the junction of the Lithonia road, which extends north-westwardly to the village of Lithonia, and the railroad leading to Atlanta. Here, beside a large log near the road, we take our first rest since leaving Freeman's. A short reverie: to be cut off or driven from one's base of supplies is always to be considered as among the most deplorable of military *contretemps*, but a voluntary permanent abandonment of the same can very rarely be justified; but we are firm in the belief that our "abandonment" and this final desperate attempt· are at least fully warranted. Our rest was a short one, after which we proceeded across the fields to the cabin of a friendly negro, who had been recommended to us as "true." We arouse him; he responds; rubs his eyes and stretches himself, and lazily yawns out that he's "mighty glad" to see us. After the usual formalities and congratulations, and additional assurances that he was really awake, the writer inquired of him, —

"Where are the Yankee forces now?"

"Dey's at Decatur, six miles dis side of Atlanta. But you'd better look sharp, honies, 'case dere's lots o' dese yere Texas rangers roaming 'bout yere huntin' runaway niggers and deserters; 'twill go mighty hard wid yer if yer cotched!"

"Don't you think we can push through?"

(Shaking his head.) "Dunno, boys; dey's pretty sharp."

"Suppose we take to the fields then, entirely?"

(Still shaking his head.) "Dunno; I 'vise yer to go back, boys; jus about impossible to git throo — Texas fellers a hard lot."

"We'll not go back, uncle; we've been back once — we're bound the other way now."

Bidding him adieu, and thanking him for his little information and poor advice, we consulted our compass with the assistance of friendly fire-flies, ascertained the direction desired, and as a mark of our profound respect for the "Texas rangers," concluded to avoid the roads altogether. We trudged onward through the fields, scaling fences, tramping through soft, muddy cornfields, fording creeks, tearing through woods and briers, until the brightening eastern sky warned us of approaching daylight of —

October 7. — Lithonia, and the Northern Georgia Railroad only three miles away! A retired spot in dense woods furnishes rest and "headquarters" for the day. We discover that we are near a log cabin, isolated from any plantation; humble habitation of the poor — second and last in the order of trust. Blacks preferred; poor whites — well, "mixed;" no sounds — nothing to indicate occupancy save the blue smoke curling gracefully from the mud-plastered chimney. We must take the risk, however, of obtaining information of the occupants. Leaving Jim in the woods, the writer circled around and cautiously approached the cabin from the opposite direction, vainly listening for sounds and watching for signs of life, but attracting no attention until reaching the very threshold of the open door. Within were a white woman with pleasant features, and several small children. They gazed speechlessly at the early-morning intruder, in apparent amazement.

The writer smilingly accosted her with, "Good morning, madam, — no cause for alarm."

"Oh!" said she, somewhat flustered, "Good morning, sir; excuse our appearance — we just got up, sir."

"Not the least consequence, madam; I just stopped to inquire if you had seen any Federals about here lately?"

"Lor' no, sir, — they've all done gone; we've more of you-uns nowadays."

"Who do you mean by 'you-uns?'"

"Why, you Confederates, what steal every thing a poor woman has got; *them's* who I mean!"

"Well, you seem to like the Yankees better than Confederates; why didn't you go off with 'em?"

"The Yankees never done me as much dirt as you-uns; they're much better-behaved folks."

"Well, madam, I'm not a Confederate — I'm a Yankee!" (She looked steadily at the writer an instant, then slowly shook her head incredulously.) Casting back over the shoulders the little gray cape which had concealed the blue, and exposing the Federal uniform to her view, the writer asked, "Well, what do you think now?" She gazed steadily at the glistening buttons and shoulder-straps which decorated the uniform, looked suspiciously into the writer's face, and suddenly responded, "No fooling, now; are you a Yankee, sure enough?" The writer assured her that he was, and briefly explained his absence from his command. She continued, "You don't *look* like our folks, nor *talk* like 'em." The writer offered additional evidence of his being a *genuine* Yankee, and the lady finally expressed herself as satisfied of the justness of his claim. Then she freely expressed herself in still stronger terms of condemnation of the Confederates, and finally declared her partiality for "blue-coats." She kindly invited the writer to "set up and take breakfast of what the Confederates have left us," which invitation was gratefully accepted. ("Twill save our rations.) During breakfast she told the writer her story of her husband, who was drafted into the rebel army, but was taken sick and died at the Confederate hospital at Chattanooga. She said, "I'm glad to say he never did 'em any good, and never fired a gun agin the old flag. I tell 'em the Yankees will whip 'em all badly yet. I don't see how it is, but by their tell the Yankees were going to be driven and driven. Our folks were always drivin' 'em, and drivin' 'em, and the Yankees kept all the time coming nearer and nearer, and now our folks have driven 'em plumb into Atlanta; there's somethin' wrong somewhere." The writer carefully observed, but recognized no indication of deception in her earnest manner, and concluded he had found another *white* person worthy of confidence and trust.

"Is this your son?" asked the writer, concerning the eldest of the children, a boy about thirteen years of age.

"Yes, sir, that's my oldest boy." (Introducing him.)

He seemed to possess the requisite amount of intelligence and gumption.

"Would you permit him to do me a favor, without betraying my secret presence here?"

"Certainly, sir; anything he can do he will do. What is it?"

"How far is it to Lithonia?"

"Wellnigh on to three mile."

"Could he go there and find out if any, and how many, Confederates are there; or if any Yankees were there lately?"

"Certainly, sir; certainly he can." The writer cautioned him: "Now be careful, my boy; don't hint to a soul that you've seen me, or a blue uniform." He gave satisfactory assurances of fidelity and secrecy, and was soon on the road to the village, receiving a motherly injunction of secrecy as a "send-off." The writer expressed his sincere thanks for the sympathy expressed and the kindness received at the hands of the lady, chatted pleasantly with the children a few moments, explained the presence of Jim in the woods as his companion and guide, and promising to return at sunset, rejoined Jim in the retreat of the forest, passing from sight eastwardly and circling around to the retreat, west of the cabin — the usual plan adopted to put "off scent" both observed and unobserved observers. The day was spent in rather gloomy reverie. Thoughts of the past flitted through the mind: terrible battle of July 22d — "hell of scenes and noises" — the ghastly dead. That the old Army of the Tennessee should be driven from its works! Extrordinary reasons, eh? Fire from the rear, and being flanked by a column charging through the railroad cut; that a portion of the line should be driven back, then, under *any* circumstances, however aggravating, leaving those who remain at their posts longest to be "gobbled." Consolation that the lost ground was immediately regained; still, that glorious fact don't restore me to my command. And comrades in the old army, and friends at home — what do they think of this mysterious absence? August 22d was one month; September 22d was two months; October 7th two months and a half. Two months and a half since a view of the old colors waving through the smoke of battle; how much brighter would they appear to me now! How did the General and balance of the staff come out of the battle? How did the old Sixth Missouri Infantry get through — officers and men, and my company? and what experiences have they all had since the battle and separation? And relatives at home — are they dead or alive? Did co-prisoners yet reach our lines and tell of my escape? A reverie of questions only; responses — blank — blank — blank! Dead to everything and everybody in the world save immediate desolate surroundings. It seems a long, long time since the battle. I wonder how they've put a fellow on the muster-rolls — "killed," "wounded," "captured," or "missing?" Oh for a safe transit to our lines! Now the long shadows of evening silently creep through the woods, and thousands of little warblers, most musical at close of day, are vieing with each other in sweet rendition of evening songs. Golden flood of sunlight; evening's balmy hour — dusk.

> "Footsteps of angels follow in her trace,
> To shut the weary eye of day in peace."

Dusky landscape; objects more and more indistinct. "Voices of the night." Nature's late evening concert — in contrast with that of the sweet warblers, who have all hushed upon the approach of night — frogs, crickets, whippoorwills.

Dark. Pursuant to promise, we repair to the friendly

cabin of the "anti-Confederate" lady for the coveted information. "Good evening;" introduction to Jim; seeking the desired information. The boy replied: —

"I only saw two Confederate cavalrymen in gray coats and pants, who were getting their horses shod at the blacksmith's; no Yankees 'bout for a long time."

Thanking the lady and her son for their kindness and interest and services, we bade them farewell, and started for the village of Lithonia. Safe — no force there; only three miles northward. Forward! No star visible but the star of hope; but the dense fog upon the earth we welcome as a friendly cover, and speed on. We have certainly marched more than three miles, but where is the village? No sounds; no lights. The trusty little compass is consulted. What! has the compass turned rebel, or does it tell us truly that we are travelling southward? A vigorous shaking fails to shake the compass from its position, and with characteristic indifference it maintains its assertion that we are facing *south*. We had followed a bend in an intersecting wood, and were unable to detect it sooner by reason of the dense fog. Negligence; what do we carry a compass for? Fog slightly clearing; log cabin near by; we approach; a rap at the door; it was slowly opened by a plainly attired lady; family inside, of ladies and children. Without explanation, the writer simply inquired for the shortest cut to the main Lithonia road. A small obscure path was pointed out as one leading directly to it, across the fields. "Thanks, madam;" off; the family somewhat agitated, crowd to the door, and peer through the darkness at our retreating forms. Headless family, as usual; wonder where all the *men* are? Rapid marching to make up for lost time constitutes our self-inflicted punishment for stupidity. The fog has risen, and we can clearly distinguish the houses of the village looming up above the foliage, in dull relief against the star-lit sky. We ascend a knoll near the suburbs, and are now in full view of the village. Halt! listen! No sounds save the barking of the faithful watch-dogs of the sleeping village, and the shrill whistle of the whippoorwills surrounding us; silent as the grave. "There's the road that will lead us straight to the railroad." To circle around the town will consume too much time, and incur greater risk of pursuit, if discovered off the road; even the dogs would bark louder at us. We determine to proceed in the middle of the road, single file — writer ahead — and march silently and rapidly for the railroad. "Time is precious, and we must reach Decatur and our lines by daybreak, only fifteen miles away." Fatigued, footsore, but determined, we proceeded in the execution of the programme, and had safely reached a point within three blocks of the coveted railroad, when two large dogs, scenting us, came into the road and barked furiously at us, while we increased our pace; one of the dogs alternately howling dismally; shortly afterward, two white men emerged into the road, both coatless, and briskly followed us, manifestly endeavoring to overtake us. The writer and Jim now marched together in the retreat, but the pursuers seemed decidedly to gain on them. Instinctively the hammer of the writer's carbine was raised with a sharp "click," and a little closer contact would have necessitated a turning and a challenge of these apparently unarmed curiosity-hunters; as it was, we succeeded in maintaining a proper distance without so dangerous an expedient. We now saw our opportunity, rapidly passed to the sidewalk, glided behind a church, swiftly over a fence or two, circled around toward the railroad, reaching another road, and thus escaped further pursuit or observation. As we now cautiously approached the railroad, we discovered before us a fire by the roadside; we pause — listen — observe. There are men about the fire; what if they should be blue-coats? Single file — stealthy approach; the tell-tale camp-fire now clearly discloses uniforms of gray. Another circling-around process through the fields, after all our pains to avoid them, and finally two tired, jaded, sore-footed, but happy and grateful *tramps* stood upon the coveted Northern Georgia Railroad, west of Lithonia — safe. "I wonder where that boy's eyes were, who told us, 'no soldiers in town?'" Jim pleaded for "rest, rest;" but there's no rest — long after midnight, and Decatur fifteen miles away. "We are on the home-stretch now, Jim, and we must completely wear ourselves out in order to reach our lines." No halting, no resting, no lagging; we are between the lines of the two armies, and daylight will find us at Decatur, or — worse. On we speed, and after a long, speechless, rapid march, in single file, north-westwardly on the railroad, we rested just a moment, and were again in rapid motion. We were now marching very rapidly, and resting but a short moment at long intervals; excellent time; buoyancy of spirits despite raw and bleeding feet. Onward! Onward! Jim, by extra effort, overtakes the writer and renews his pleading for rest, muttering "I's worn out; I can't stand dis; my feet's gin out," etc. Pleading "overruled;" there's no halt — no rest; half running, leaping along from tie to tie, like steeds fresh from the stable. Now grand old Stone Mountain looms up against the dim-lit western sky; we rapidly approach — we pass it. On, on we flee, until speed is finally lessened by caution — an object ahead; it's a frame house immediately beside the track. Slackened speed — stealthy approach — a halt. We listen; no sounds but our own labored breathing. We rest — stretching our weary, worn frames on the track-bed, and relieving our raw, blistered, and bleeding feet from the weight of our bodies for a moment, preparatory to the fresh undertaking before us; then up, and cautiously onward again, slowly, in single file, approaching the suspected hut beside the track. A sharp turn in the railroad freed us from gloomy timber, but suddenly disclosed a camp-fire. An exceedingly cautious investigation disclosed a railroad-cut, with the banks of earth extending upward on both sides of the track ten or twelve feet; the house loomed up beyond it; the fire was on the opposite summit of the hillock, near the opening made by the cut; suspicion that it's a picket-post commanding the railroad. A slow, cautious approach of the writer on "all-fours" to a favorable position, which discloses that around the fire lie men in gray uniforms — that's quite sufficient for our purpose. Too tired and foot-sore to undertake the customary tedious and circuitous route around them, and deriving much comfort in the belief that it is the Confederate outpost, we determined to pass *beneath* them. The situation was fully explained in whispers to Jim, who was doubly cautioned of danger and of the necessity of absolute silence, and the novel adventure began. Single file, fifteen feet apart — on "all-fours" — the writer leading, the two slowly and silently entered the gloomy cut; arose, hugged the earthen bank, and safely passed twelve feet beneath the drowsy sentries. We reached a safe position west of the fire, somewhat worse for slimy mud, and halted opposite the house we had seen before seeing the fire. It seems a safe distance from the picket-post, and was separated from it by a small ravine and the railroad; not a sound from it — still and dark as the grave. But morning is rapidly approaching; our chances are desperate. Leaving Jim beside the railroad track, the writer stepped to the door, listened a moment, then knocked. Sepulchral echoes only responded. He knocked again, and louder, instinctively glancing in the direction of the picket-fire, to detect any commotion about it. A rustle inside — signs of life. A gentleman in "undress uniform" partially opened the door, and inquired rather gruffly: —

"Well, what's wanting?"

"Captain, how near is our picket-post here to the Yankees?"

"Why, they're at Decatur yet; their pickets are about a mile this side, on the railroad."

"Are you sure of that, Captain?"

"Well, they were there last night, for I see'd 'em."

Information considered reliable, and the writer turned to leave, inwardly congratulating himself that he had not been placed under the military necessity of prevarication, pleasantly saying: "Thank you, sir — sorry to disturb you, Captain;" when the other rather authoritatively blurted out, "Well, see 'ere, stranger — who are you, anyhow?" The writer, harsh in manner, but rather frightened at the *bottom*, promptly replied, "Capt. Blake, of the Thirty-fifth Georgia; and I want correct information, and if you mislead us, down will come your house — understand?" "Oh, it's jest as I tell you, Captain; you'll find it so, Captain" (evidently swallowing the bait). The writer anxiously peered toward the quiet, undisturbed picket-post; then Jim was rejoined in a twinkle, and away we joyfully flew Atlantaward — "by rail!" Decatur only four miles away! Who our informant was, whether soldier or hoosier, we know not and care not. A mile-heat, and Jim renews his fretting at the hardship: "Dis is too swift for my feet." But there was no slackening of speed, no rest; away we speeded, greatly stimulated by the latest intelligence, and vainly endeavoring to forget the burning, itching, and scalding sensations produced by torn and bloody feet; leaping cheerfully from tie to tie, Jim piteously urging, "I *can't* keep up — no use talking — *can't do it!*" We halt for a moment, only to again urge upon Jim the absolute necessity of *wearing our feet out* in the attempt to reach our lines and safety — *only three miles away!* The writer's feet were causing him great pain — burning, scalding, smarting, itching — not a spot an inch square of nature's covering on either foot; and the hard, irritating leather of his boots, reddened by frequent wettings and exposure, mercilessly lacerated the already torn and bleeding flesh; their cruel harshness but partially softened and appeased by the free offerings of *bloody feet!* Yet, what could he do? He could not travel over the gravelled road-bed nor through the fields barefoot; nothing can be gained by tearing still more the lacerated flesh by pulling them off and on. There's but *one* conclusion — there's no relief outside the Federal lines.

The brightening eastern sky reminds us of rapidly approaching day; yet on with the march — we must reach Decatur at any cost. On, on — limping and desperately struggling westward! Brighter and brighter grows the early morning; it is dawn. Broad daylight now steals upon us like an unwelcome guest, but still onward; sunrise — "Old Sol" sheds forth his golden rays over the landscape; but still onward, onward! We can now see through the timber the houses of Decatur — glorious sight!

We're only one mile from town; but where are our outposts? Still on and on we limp, and struggle, and stagger, in desperation and hope. We now joyfully see our breastworks; no sounds — no sights — smoke curling gracefully from behind them up through the foliage; somebody must be there. Suddenly our attention is called to the mysterious conduct and stealthy actions of two white men near a residence to the south of us, and about an eighth of a mile from the railroad — one in gray, the other in butternut; one approaches the other from the timber, and receives a small package; breakfast (?); they seem unmindful of us, who still continue our limping march in full view. Whoever they are, they seem harmless, and their apparent timidity is our encouragement. Now we enter the Federal fortifications extending across the railroad, a quarter of a mile east of the town, and find they are *vacated* — camp-fires still smoking, but the Federals gone. Smiling Hope had beckoned us on, only to make despair the more certain. The coveted Federal lines at last, and nothing to greet us but the refuse of a camp and the smouldering remnants of camp-fires which were kindled by friends! Despondent — hungry — foot-sore — cheated — exhausted — chafed — irritated — lacerated — drooping in the gloom of fading hopes.

> "Weary of living, so weary;
> Longing to lie down and die!"

Slowly, sadly, and silently we limp through the familiar scenes of an abandoned camp, select a secluded nook in the timber beyond it, and establish "headquarters" for the day on the bank of a pearly little brooklet which had furnished the prior occupants of the camp with water. To proceed further seemed an absolute impossibility; with great difficulty, causing great pain, was Jim able to pull the hardened boots from the writer's swollen and bleeding feet. Thus we considered ourselves established for —

October 8. — To remain here we knew would be extra hazardous, but to depart — impossible.

"Well, Jim," said the writer, despairingly, while bathing his lacerated feet in the cool, flowing water of the little rivulet, and breaking a long, gloomy silence, "you'd better sleep while I keep guard; you can take a good, long sleep, and then watch while I sleep." Jim was agreeable, and in an incredibly short period the immediate vicinity became resonant with most unearthly snoring — sufficient to raise the dead! "Poor Jim," thought the writer, as he viewed his prostrate form; "he thought it would be fun to follow a Yankee to our lines." It was neither sacrifice, nor preference, nor lot that secured for Jim the first sleep after our "crowning effort." For the writer, pain prohibited sleep, though the cooling ripples of the streamlet manifestly allayed inflammation and considerably lessened suffering. While Jim slept, his companion in misery sat gloomily, half thinking, half dreaming; and while the refreshing waters played gratefully around his lacerated, useless feet, the tide of grief seemed fast rising to overwhelm him. Bitter, bitter disappointment touches the eyelids, and *other* streamlets copiously flow to the music of the gurgling rivulet. Morning dew-drops still linger, sparkling on the surrounding foliage, and —

> "Tears are hung on every tree:
> For thus my gloomy fantasy
> Makes all things weep with me."

As the writer sat thus sadly musing, he observed a boy of about thirteen approach, and suddenly start off in another direction. He wears a full Federal uniform. Is he really a friend? or did he discover us, and now retreats to spread the secret? Such suspense and uncertainty not to be willingly endured. Oh, the wonderfully attractive power of blue cloth! The writer was desperate enough to trust in the deceptive cloth alone; he limpingly approached the wearer of it — barefooted, bareheaded, coatless — and overtook and hailed the youth in blue. He turned, apparently much surprised, and gazed at the coatless, hatless challenger, and looked sympathetically at his swollen, bleeding feet. The writer inquired: —

"Who are you, my friend?"

"I'm a native here, sir — don't belong to the army."

"What are you doing with that uniform on, then?"

"I was employed by Lieut. ———, quartermaster on Gen. Cox's staff, Twentieth Army Corps."

"Gen. Cox of the Federal army?"

"Yes, sir."

"Whereabouts?"

"Here in Decatur, sir, where they were stationed."

"When did they leave, bub?" (Patronizingly.)

"Dunno; sometime last night. They were here last night and gone this morning; that's all I know, sir." (Torturing information.)

"Do you know what I am, bub?" (Smiling.)

"Oh yes, sir; I know you're a Federal by your blue pants."

"Are you friendly to the Federals?"

"Yes, sir; always was friendly."

"Well, you see I'm in distress; will you do me the favor of finding out for me whether the Federals have left Atlanta too, if possible, by inquiring around Decatur and bringing me word here at dark to-night?"

"Yes, sir; I'll do all I can for you." (Casting piteous glances at the worthless feet.) "I'll find out, sir."

"Now let me caution you, bub, not to speak of my presence here to a living soul; can I trust you for that?"

"Yes, sir; you can trust me. I won't tell, sir."

"Well, I rely upon your honor now, and trust you."

"You can trust me, sir. I'll be back near dark."

And nodding adieu, he was soon lost to view through the woods. Alas! that forced interview. It was now after noon, by sun; the writer painfully limped back to "headquarters," and awakening Jim, apprised him of what had occurred. We then took the usual precaution to change our "headquarters," whence we could, unobserved, observe any approach to the old one. The writer's turn now came to welcome sleep. Feet less painful, but fearfully swollen. How far did we march last night? Let's see: three miles to Lithonia, three miles out of our way and return — that's six and three are nine, and fifteen to Decatur — that's twenty-four, and at least three measured in circling around the village and obstacles — that's twenty-seven miles; equal at least to thirty-seven under favorable circumstances. Jim agrees fully.

"Now, Jim, remember and shake me well upon the least suspicious sound or sight; keep your ears and eyes wide open; we're in a dangerous place, but we have this little breech-loader (carbine), and can, if necessary, force a halt of any thing short of a *crowd* at a respectful distance, if you 'waken me in time. Now be cautious, Jim."

"Oh, I'm suttain to do it — suttain to do it."

The writer placed the loaded carbine beside him, propped his feet up from the ground, and almost instantly became unconscious in the soothing embrace of sweet sleep. Alas, alas! that sleep. Fitful dreams of armies, and woods, and negroes, restored feet, home and friends, passed through the mind of the exhausted sleeper, who had placed implicit reliance in the diligence of his rested companion, until he was suddenly awakened by an exclamation, in a loud tone of voice, "Halloo, there!"

Opening his eyes, he beheld, standing at his feet, a man in a butternut uniform — double-breasted coat, with two rows of brass buttons, slouch hat, and wild eye. "My God! my God! what does this mean?" He took deliberate aim down the barrel of his rifle at the motionless writer's breast, and excitedly demanded, "Surrender?" The writer looked the excited butternut square in the face, but uttered not a word. "Where is Jim?" Slightly turning his head, he observed another person, in a Federal uniform, armed with a rifle, and standing guard over Jim, a few yards distant. (Disparaging compound of mystification and mortification. "How did this happen?")

"Well," asked the butternut, "what do you say?"

"Am I to be treated as a prisoner of war, sir?"

"Oh, certainly, sir; most assuredly, sir."

"Well, I see no alternative; I'm your prisoner, sir."

Now, how did this happen? Turning to Jim, the writer, perhaps rather sharply, inquired:

"Jim, how did this happen?"

"Well, Lieutenant, you might a-known I'd fall asleep when de *warm sun* struck me." Indignation at white heat, threatening to burst the bands of poor concealment; but indignation cannot restore freedom; anger cannot mend affairs. Well, discretion may "take the reins" if it can hold the team. But Jim fell asleep; Jim, who has slept all morning; Jim, who was fully apprised of danger; Jim, who was "certain to watch." "Ah! Jim, Jim, that confidence could be so misplaced in you!" The butternut now gathered the writer's carbine, carefully examined it, replaced the cap with one of his own, and seemed more at ease. The writer said:

"That cap was not put on to miss fire, sir."

"Likely, but I'd rather trust one of my own."

The following conversation then substantially occurred, which the writer feels certain will be recognized as correct by all who heard or participated in it. The butternut was the spokesman; the one in blue was evidently subordinate, and simply "seconded motions." Said the former to the writer, —

"What is your rank, sir — and regiment?"

"First Lieutenant, A. D. C. on Second Division staff, Fifteenth Army Corps; my regiment is the Sixth Missouri Infantry."

"From Missouri, eh? That's one of our States, and you fighting on the other side, eh?

"That's hardly fair, sir. Missouri fought herself into the Union, although a slave State, and those on the Union side think she deserves all the more credit for it. Missouri's my native State; I'm not ashamed of her record in this war."

"You say you were born in Missouri?"

"Yes, sir — in St. Louis."

The two captors smiled at each other incredulously.

"What's your name?"

"Bailey's my name, sir — and yours?"

"Foster." The one in blue looked suddenly and sharply around at "Foster" — had he inadvertently given his real name?

But in subsequent conversation, why was the name of "Fowler" substituted for that of "Foster" by the unreserved "boy in blue?" The stupid disclosure of the latter is considered superior authority to the guarded answer of "Foster," hence our hero in butternut will be designated as "Fowler."

Since the recapture, the writer's almost uncontrollable indignation boiled at the sight of that blue uniform. It found partial vent when he turned sharply to the wearer and asked:

"What do you think would become of you, sir, if caught by our troops engaged in this business in a blue uniform?" With guilty look he replied: "Well, in the first place, sir, I don't intend to be caught; this is our business, you know."

"Very questionable and dangerous sort of business."

A new light dawned upon the writer's mind as he mused: "This blue uniform was to be used as decoy to capture me, if awake; it was to entice to a 'friend' only to disclose a treacherous foe."

"Our business" to prowl about under false colors, to gain some mean advantage over deceived and unsuspecting victims. Void of manly courage which would present the *soldier* at the front, the "business" of decoying the unwary restrains cowardly souls to the rear.

> "Wears friendship's mask for purposes of spite,
> Fawns in the day, and butchers in the night;
> With the cold caution of a coward's spleen,
> Which fears not guilt, but always seeks a screen."

Let the reader receive a more satisfactory introduction to these reconcilers of the "blue and gray."

"Fowler"—About five feet eight inches in height, well proportioned; light auburn hair; rather long, flowing, sandy beard; mustache; piercing, light blue eyes; slouch felt hat; voice rather pleasant (except when it first aroused the writer with unwelcome summons to surrender). Grayish-brown or butternut Confederate uniform — double breasted coat, with two rows of brass buttons; manner — rough, firm, and uncouth. "Ornament," — breech-loading Henry rifle. His portrait in this volume represents him with his mustache and much of his beard shorn, but the same lovely features are there — the same noble countenance, the same angelic expression, the same tender, pathetic look, the same meek and lamb-like expression of the soft blue eyes — all of which so *captivated* the writer in 1864, and which, doubtless, will tempt the appreciative admiration, especially of those who can bring to their aid the interesting science of *physiognomy*.

The "boy in blue" we will introduce as one who disgraces the honorable name of "Singleton." How do I know? That's immaterial for present purposes; it is sufficient that it's a *fact*. He seemed to be about five feet nine inches in height; dark and rather short hair; large black eyes; black hat; dressed in a complete and apparently not much worn Federal infantry uniform; decidedly unbecoming in blue! "Ornament" — a United States Springfield rifle, calibre 69. (Did he get the "ornament" where he got the blue uniform?)

"FOWLER."

"What are you doing with this nigger here?" asked Fowler, referring to terrified Jim. The writer replied:

"He knows the country and roads, and I accepted his services as my guide. He has been here before, I believe." Turning to the frightened negro, Fowler inquired of him:

"Where did you come from, boy?" (Presuming on association with the writer, doubtless, Jim promptly responded:)

"I c'sider my home in St. Louis, sar."

"How did you get 'way down here, then?"

"Come down wid Lieutenant dar — wid de army."

"How'd you get inside our lines?" (That's a poser!)

"Wid Lieutenant dar, sar." (Fowler seemed puzzled.)

Jim's adeptness as a prudent *liar* took the writer completely by surprise, and thinking that perhaps the life of the "nigger" might depend on it, the writer attempted to rescue him by explaining: "He don't mean he was a *soldier*, sir; he means to say that he came down with me from St. Louis as my *servant*, and that he was captured with me at the battle of Atlanta — is that it, Jim?"

"Dat's it, sar, zactly," said Jim quickly, jumping at the suggestion like a trout at a fly.

"So you were taken prisoner before Atlanta, were you, sir?" asked Fowler of the writer.

"I was, sir, — the day Gen. McPherson was killed."

"Where have you been ever since that time?"

"Part of the time a prisoner,— the other part trying to get back." (Glances indicating incredulity.)

It must be borne in mind that Jim had been a "runaway nigger" for more than a year, and, like the writer, was a "gemman of de woods," entirely dependent for aid and comfort upon the charity and good-will of sympathizing strangers; but he voluntarily undertook, and perhaps wisely, to conceal these facts from our captors; and the writer recognized the "military necessity" of having his *story* appear consistent, and experienced considerable relief when he had succeeded in diverting attention from the "d—d nigger."

Fowler now placed Singleton on guard, while he proceeded to search the prisoner for "contraband of war." The writer kindly assisted him. The maps of the country printed on linen were passed as dirty handkerchiefs, by dexterously exposing only the unprinted sides. (How thankful was the prisoner that he had presented his watch and other valuables to his friends further south.) After viewing the valueless "assets," he remarked, "All I want now is the pocket-book — best one I've seen for some time; the other things you may keep a while longer." ("*A while longer?*" What does he mean by that? Possible?) First flash of suspicion of intended foul play — ominous glances. "Well, you may fix up now to go with us."

The prisoner donned his coat, and after much pain succeeded in pulling his hardened boots on his lacerated feet, and endeavored to obey the peremptory orders of his captors; he *limped* obedience. The party marched to the abandoned Federal earthworks in single file — Singleton, in blue, leading; then came the writer, then Jim, then Fowler bringing up the rear, and carrying his own and the captured rifle — one on each shoulder. As we neared the works, the writer recognized the boy in the Federal uniform with whom he had conversed in the morning, and who had so faithfully promised not to betray him. He was accompanied by another boy of about his age, and both seemed to have been interested spectators of the capture from a safe distance. The writer hailed his morning friend with, "Well, young man, you *betrayed* me, didn't you?"

"No, sir; I didn't," he replied.

"Who did?"

"This feller." (Pointing to his companion.)

"Well, who told him?"

"I did," said he, rather hesitatingly.

"Well, didn't you promise me faithfully" —

"There — stop that," said Fowler, savagely; "don't ask that boy any more questions; do you understand that?" (The prisoner thought he did.)

We passed beyond the breastworks, eastwardly, and

had gone but a short distance when Fowler (rear guard) hailed Singleton (advance guard), remarking, with an illy concealed wink, "We must turn this cuss over to our cavalry, and get rid of him before dark."

Singleton, with a knowing look, nodded assent.

"Where is the cavalry post?" the writer ventured to inquire.

"At the Circle," responded Fowler.

"The 'Circle?' Where's that, sir?"

"You'll find out soon enough."

(Another significant exchange of glances between the "guards.") We had now cleared the open space in front of our abandoned works, and halted at a beautiful spring of clear water. Our guards lay on the ground alternately and drank; so did Jim. Fowler said to the writer, "You'd better get down and drink, sir; you won't get water again right away." (Glancing at Singleton.) The writer was thirsty enough, but an indescribable *something* restrained him from accepting the invitation. "Thank you; I'm not very thirsty." (More significant glances.) We continue the march. "My feet pain me so, gentlemen, that I must ask you to move slower; you see I can hardly limp along with you." Fowler responded, "Never mind; *you won't want to use 'em much longer.*" ('That settles it; they are going to shoot us! no mistaking the meaning of *that* remark.

Yes, at last we feel that it is "possible;" this is their "business," in which they earn their *arms and blue uniforms.*)

> "Within the hollow, sighing woods
> A vague, mysterious sadness broods."

Singleton now turned to Fowler and remarked, with an inquiring look, "We can cut across the woods here to the road, eh?"

"Yes," responded the latter, and we penetrated the thick woods, changing direction until well advanced therein, when there occurred another exchange of glances between the front and rear of our little column, followed by a halt.

(Has the critical moment arrived?) Fowler sharply remarked to Singleton, "See 'ere," and both moved apart from their prisoners for consultation. Now, if my feet were not useless, how I'd lessen the distance between us; but — helpless — *hopeless!* "Jim," said the writer (*sotto voce*), "they're *bent on killing us* — they're certainly *bent on killing us!*" (Jim's eyes opened wide; he looked wild.) "There's but *one* thing left for us to do, Jim; we *must* fight!" (Jim slightly shook his head.) "Then we must die like *dogs*, without an effort. No! no! let's take the *last chance.*"

Fowler now stealthily approached from behind us, manifestly endeavoring to steal the purport of our conversation, but the writer immediately turned it on to affairs at St. Louis. Other similar attempts resulted the same. It was impossible for them to consult privately without according to us the same privilege, and *we knew it*. Their consultation was renewed — so was ours. "We're enough for 'em, Jim," urged the writer, encouragingly. "I'll grab the rifle ahead, as he carries it over his shoulder, and if I don't knock him over with it, I'll hold on to it tightly, so he can't shoot us; and when I grab, the man behind will shoot me immediately, if *you don't stop him!* Will you let him shoot me, Jim?"

"No, sir; I won't let him shoot you."

"Will you *turn on him*, Jim, and *stick to him,* — *hold on to him* so he can't shoot, until I can come to you, or you to me?"

"I see, I see," said Jim, excitedly. "I's *suttain* to do it — *suttain* to do it." (But will he?)

"When you see my hands flap on both sides, look out, and be ready, Jim; that will be the signal to grab."

"I's suttain to do it, Lieutenant; you may 'pend on me *dis time,* — suttain sure to do it."

"We can't be any *worse* off, Jim; and by this we may be better off."

"I see, I see; you may 'pend I'll do it."

"Here they come, Jim. Now, *strike quick and strong.*"

The double conference being over, we resumed our march through the thick woods, as before, — Singleton leads the column, the writer following him; then came Jim, followed by Fowler. Singleton carried his rifle loosely and carelessly over his shoulder, within easy reach of the writer; Fowler carried a rifle on each shoulder. With stealthy glances, the writer determined the exact band upon which his first grasp should tighten. Beyond the rise in the ground, a few feet ahead, the struggle *must* begin. We reach the knoll, and gradually descend into the little valley beyond, — "the valley of death." (?) How the thoughts crowd through the mind. Feeling of *dread*. Success of one party — certain death of the other; which will it be? Begin at that sapling there, — "No! no! more delay; not quite yet, — just one moment longer. Could I but *tear loose* from this invisible *restraining demon!*" Here is a good spot — "wait?" "Don't lose the opportunity, — don't wait. *Will Jim do his duty?* Our *lives* depend on that! Trust him — try him; he's *awake* now. Do they notice my agitation? No more excuses, — no more hesitation; be quick, — be strong. *Strike!*"

> "A mighty yearning, like the first
> Fierce impulse unto crime!"

The eye is fixed upon the band of the rifle; the writer increases his limping pace, closing right up to the unsuspecting leader. Now! now! "Just beyond this stump, and I *will!*" All the powers of soul and body are pledged and concentrated for the desperate work;

the hands flap the tardy signal,—lo! the scene changes. We halt. All advantages still retained by the captors; stupid delay; *cowardly* hesitation; golden opportunity lost — lost — lost. Singleton turned and exchanged significant glances with Fowler. "What if we were mistaken as to their intentions? *Some* lives would have been sacrificed to no purpose." We were not long kept in the possibility of doubt. Fowler stood the captured carbine against a stump, coolly cocked his rifle, and, looking the writer steadily in the face, said (how well he remembers — how the words were *burned* into the tablet of his memory): "My friend, this is as good a place to die as any man could wish." There was a choking sensation for an instant, as the writer fully realized the significance of the solemn words, but quickly rallying, he inquired:

"Why am I to be killed, sir? Didn't you promise to treat me as a prisoner of war?"

"Well, this is the way we treat *our* prisoners of war."

The writer looked him steadily, full in the face, speechless, for a long moment, and for an instant he seemed not a little annoyed by the silent rebuke, but suddenly resumed:

"You are a d—d Yankee; and the d—d Yankees stole my wife's skillet, and I'll have no mercy on 'em. You've got to die, sir." (Peculiar sensations.) "But many acts were done in both armies that the officers did not approve of. It's very hard, sir, that I must die for the act of one of our soldiers, committed while I was a prisoner in your lines, and of which I could not have any knowledge or control. Here, I'll give you papers which I think will protect you against such depredations in future. Besides, sir, the act was not murder; the offence don't merit such punishment as this." "I don't care, sir; papers don't protect; even Gen. Sherman gave papers that didn't protect; I'll fix you, d—n you, and then I'll be better satisfied." (Shallow pretext in the absence of a cause. The sheep striving to argue the wolf out of his supper.) "This is very hard, sir, — very hard; my relatives and friends will never know what became of me." Turning to Singleton: "Can't you have something to say in my behalf, sir? I have done nothing to deserve such treatment as this. Do you approve of this, sir? Can't you intercede to prevent deliberate murder?" Singleton seemed touched by the earnest appeal to his manhood; gazed pitifully at the writer with his great black eyes a moment, then hung and slowly shook his head. (Evidently a struggle within him between a sense of right and wrong, and of his incurred obligation to Fowler.) Driven to utter desperation, the writer proposed to take his surrendered carbine, with *one* round of ammunition, any distance, and decide his right to live, in a rifle duel with the best marksman of the two captors; well knowing that if this appeal to their courage and chivalry proved successful, he could fortify himself behind a tree, and bid them defiance with the *several rounds of ammunition still concealed on his person* and several dry caps still in his vest pocket. The proposition was scouted at once, and seemed to furnish Singleton with an excuse for smothering even the slight sympathy he had previously evinced.

"D—n him," said he, "he wants to fight."

Singleton then asked Fowler (*sotto voce*):

"What'll we do with him after we shoot him?"

"Bury the cuss," calmly replied Fowler.

"But we've nothing to dig with," suggested Singleton.

"Oh! well, ther're plenty of leaves, — the hogs will take care of the rest;" then turning to the writer, unaware that he had heard the interesting conversation, Fowler very considerately said:

"We'll bury you, sir, if we can, — if that's any consolation for you." The writer was silent.

Nothing will answer but *blood*. Reason baffled — arguments impotent — appeals vain — hope fled — crushing despair! To die in battle — to fall at the front — what a luxury compared to this; but for this was I born, — to this have I come at last; face it, then, like a *soldier!* The writer folded his arms and slowly bowed his head — hopeless.

He saw nothing — he felt nothing but heavy pulsations beating like a muffled drum; he heard nothing but his own labored breathing; he hurriedly thought of home and friends far away, and then solemnly of the great, mysterious future, — and was ready to die. Why this delay? He raised his eyes and beheld the trio before him steadily gazing at him; firmness, hatred, and determination seemed depicted on the two white countenances, sympathy and pity on the black. A suggestion suddenly flashed through his mind: take the *very last* chance — run! Foolhardy attempt. He rapidly mused: "If I stand, I'll be killed; if I run, it cannot be worse; there's a *chance* one way, none the other. If I can surprise them by a sudden and unexpected movement, it will serve to unsteady their aim, as the sudden spring or flight of game unsteadies the aim of the sportsman; beside, I can run zig-zag, which will all the more confuse them." Do it! do it! The writer, as if unwittingly, slowly turned his head carelessly, and in an instant surveyed the ground behind him. The observant Singleton instantly remarked:

"He's fixing to run!" Fowler responded:

"Let him run, — let's see how far he'll get?"

"Ah," said the writer, "it's too late to run now; I can hardly walk, even had I chance to run. But — but would you give me twenty steps?"

"No, sir!" emphatically replied Fowler.

"Ten?" asked the writer.

"No, sir, — not an inch."

On one or two occasions, as Mr. Fowler will well rememher, as the writer inadvertently stepped toward him, he brought his rifle down, like a zealous sentry, and presented it to the writer's body, warning him not to "undertake any of his Yankee tricks." More than once the prisoner half expected to feel the sting of his rifle-ball. Fowler finally said:

"Well, sir, we've fooled away enough time with you, and now if you want to pray a little, you have a moment or two to do it." (Casting a significant glance at Singleton.)

"Thanks, sir; thanks." (It's manifestly too late to pray "deliver us from evil;" God helps those who help themselves. Heartless, bloodthirsty brutes.)

"Your time is a'most up already," urged Fowler; "you must hurry." (That evaded, dreaded moment is being rapidly forced forward.)

To allay suspicion of his intention, the writer rested one knee on the ground. Instantly Fowler's glance flashed to Singleton, and both rifles bore upon the writer's breast. He comprehended the predetermined programme to shoot him in that position, in a flash, and immediately arose and demanded the promised "two minutes."

"You've had 'em, — you've had 'em, d—n you," said Fowler, whose lips were now bloodless and quivering with excitement. "Kneel there!" demanded he, staring wildly at the prisoner, whose thoughts were now all behind him. Quick! the dreaded instant is *here*.

The writer bent his knees as if to kneel, but only to spring. Quick as a flash, he suddenly sprang backward, and turning, fled at full speed, maintaining a zig-zag motion which was exceedingly creditable to his lacerated feet, that responded nobly to the call upon them to assist in one last, desperate effort to place their possessor beyond the range of hostile rifles. Of course, the spring was the signal to fire, and fire they did! Three shots were fired at the retreating form of the prisoner (?) in rapid succession, and a fourth later.

The first was from the rifle of Fowler, and while the writer was hardly five feet from its muzzle. He felt the hot breath of the rifle almost scorching his left cheek. "Missed!" Excellent marksman, — too far to the left, brother Fowler.

The second was from the "U. S. Springfield" in the hands of Singleton, in blue, when the writer had gained some fifteen feet in distance. Calmer than Fowler, his aim was more accurate, despite the zig-zag feature maintained by the retreating form. The large rifle-ball struck the *mark*, and the writer was instantly and violently hurled to the earth, — so violently, that it seemed to him as though the earth arose and struck him in the face. A deadly quiver was felt for an instant, and the right arm (penning these lines) fell paralyzed and useless to the ground. "There goes my arm," thought the writer, but the ball had penetrated *deeper;* it passed through the body and right scapula (shoulder-blade), penetrating the right lung, shattering an upper rib, and baring the subclavian artery in its passage. The hot blood spirted out fearfully; but no sooner down than up. The third shot must have been from the writer's captured carbine in the hands of Fowler; and just as he was rising (he knows not how), the third report rang through the woods, and he felt his cap suddenly leave his head, and *flying blue cloth* indicated how near the ball came to the mark. There is a possibility that the credit for marksmanship, accorded to Singleton in the confusion of the moment and rapid firing, belongs to Fowler, but the large size of the wound seems to confirm the impression that the credit belongs to the "boy in blue." But up, up, and on he flew, holding the helpless right arm up with the left, as the speed was increased, and all pains forgotten in the flight for life. At every pulsation the blood spirted fitfully from the gaping wound, and the writer, with excited misgivings, heard the ominous gurgle of the ebbing life-current as it freely bathed the right side of his body, and clotted in his hardened boot. "Three rifles — three shots," and additional relief came with the abandonment of the difficult zig-zag feature of the flight. Another shot! Where from? Reloaded? Impossible! The ball harmlessly scatters the leaves a safe distance from the writer. Distance between ex-captors and ex-captive now lengthens rapidly, but a slight turn of the head detects dreaded sounds of *pur-*

THE SHOOTING IN THE WOODS.

suit. Speed was still more increased; effort was put forth to the very utmost; all the powers of the failing body were urged to retain the advantage gained. On like the wind, with the determination to spend the last particle of strength, the last drop of blood, for the precious privilege of *dying* free from the grasp of the bloodthirsty fiends. But the speed was suddenly slackened, instinctively, at the call of a familiar voice ringing through the woods, "Lieutenant! O Lieutenant! *Please* wait for me!" 'Twas Jim! He shortly after overtook the writer, and seemed overjoyed, exclaiming, "I nebber, nebber seed a thing done so quick as dat in all my life. Gemmen, dat beats de debil!" After he had recovered his breath sufficiently to heed something beyond his own excited utterances, he suddenly seemed to suspect the writer's condition, and looking intently into his blanched face, asked:

"Why, Lieutenant, are you hurt?"

"Yes, badly hurt, I guess; didn't you see me fall?"

"Yes, but I thought you just stumbled; you got up so quick, I 'cluded you wasn't hurt." Looking wildly at the torn and bloody coat, he asked:

"Where, Lieutenant?"

"I thought it was only my arm at first, but I see it's deeper (glancing at the torn coat-breast); I don't dare look yet. How did you get away, Jim?"

"When dey emptied all de guns on you, you think I'se

gwine to stay wid 'em, — who, *me?* No, sir. Dey fired one shot after I left; wasn't time to load, — must a' had a pistol or 'volver too, I reckon, eh?"

"Did they fire at you too?"

"Dunno, — didn't hit me if dey did; must a' fired at me tho'. My Lord! you was done gone in a jiff!"

"Well, Jim, didn't they try to follow us?"

"No-o-o, sir! What! ketch you? You was done gone, I tell yer, — clean gone out o' sight in a flash."

The writer could hardly suppress laughter at the enthusiasm of his excited companion, and the effort caused expectoration. What! Blood? and the moisture about the mouth bloody, too? No mistake — bleeding at the mouth.

"Jim, we must get away from here. They'll expect us to go for the railroad, or north-west toward Atlanta, so we'll go south. Let's see the compass? (Examines it.) You can help me over the fences, Jim; I feel I'm badly hurt."

Now, the other living witnesses to what occurred during our short acquaintance in the woods, if so disposed, can fully corroborate what is herein stated. Call Mr. Fowler — call Mr. Singleton.

We were now about a mile from the scene of "battle," whence we rapidly walked perhaps two miles further southwardly, when the writer's failing strength compelled a halt. Ghastly, and weak, and bleeding; overcome with excitement, fatigue, and great loss of blood, he suddenly became dizzy, reeled an instant, and fell to the ground. "Water! Jim, water!" Jim ran quickly to a neighboring brook and returned with a canteen of cool, refreshing water, of which the fainting soldier drank eagerly; after which Jim kindly bathed his forehead, looking pitifully into the pale features, while tear-drops rapidly chased each other down his black cheeks. He finally asked, imploringly, "Lieutenant, can you eber forgive Jim for dropping asleep dat time?" (Tears flowing faster.)

"Yes, Jim; promise you'll never speak of it again?"

"Thanks, Lieutenant. But oh! you look so sick."

"Jim, that was a *bad* shot; and if I should die, tell the Federals, if you reach them, how this happened. Give them my name — Bailey — Morgan L. Smith's staff." The writer also requested that some one write to his friends, giving their address.

"Now, will you remember all this, Jim?" (Jim nodded assent.)

"Sure, Jim?" (Continued nodding.)

The eyesight of the wounded soldier grew dimmer and dimmer; objects grew more and more indistinct; the questions were presented: "Is this really death? The great *mystery* mine?" There was a lingering, dreamy realization of passing existence, weary eyelids slowly closed o'er willing eyes, followed by a gradual soothing relapse into—oblivion. He slumbered, he knows not how long, but when he awoke it was sunset; the lustreless eyes slowly opened, and beheld a flood of golden light streaming through the tree tops, gilding and tinting the foliage with royal beauty, while the calm sunset hour was musical with sweet warblings of merry songsters, that flitted among the branches. Beautiful! — beautiful! he thought, as he struggled for an instant to recall the reason of his presence here, and half doubting that he was still upon the earth. The dreamy reverie was interrupted by the voice of Jim, inquiring:

" How do you feel, Lieutenant?"

The writer was cold and numb, and stiff in every joint. Free expectoration of blood. The place where the body had rested was marked and discolored with dark, clotted blood-stains. Jim assisted the writer to a sitting posture. Sinking, faint sensation; gradual full realization of the facts. Jim had gathered some sugar-corn from a neighboring field, and after appropriating the juice of four stalks, the wounded man seemed greatly revived, and the sickening, faint sensation ceased. In his weakness, he imagined he could make Atlanta, over ten miles away, without difficulty; and it now being near twilight, he insisted upon starting out on the march for the railroad northwestwardly. He had proceeded but a few yards, when he was compelled to realize the great change of an hour; he suddenly fainted, and again drooped unconscious to the earth. The cool water soon revived him, and, against Jim's friendly protest, he again persisted in making the vain attempt, leaning upon the strong arm of his companion. How easy it would be even to die within the Federal lines. "Jim, let me spend my last strength in the effort to reach there." "But, Lieutenant, you're so sick that"—"Hist! What sounds are those?" Nearer—nearer. We silently crouch behind friendly foliage, while on a by-road, hardly fifteen feet away, passes a squadron of Confederate cavalry. We distinctly see their carbines and gray uniforms, and hear their clanking sabre-scabbards. Jim, at first, was disposed to beat a rapid retreat, but was silently borne to the ground by the clinging form of his wounded companion. The excitement created by this narrow escape served in still another way to convince the writer of his weakness and inability to reach the Federal lines. At this moment his eye rested on a light streaming from a residence but a short distance down the road. "How its beams seem to beckon me!" There was a moment's silence, broken by the writer with, "Jim, no use talking; I believe I'm mortally wounded. But if I'm mistaken, Jim, that light—that house—whatever it is—is my last chance for life. I know I can't live in the woods through this night. I *know* it. Take me to that house."

"But, Lieutenant, 'spose they should be rebels?"

"Never mind, Jim; they are *human beings*, anyway. Take me there — take me there."

"But 'spose they should tell their cavalry?"

"'Spose nothing, Jim; take me there, or *I'll go alone.*"

Leaning on Jim's friendly arm, the wounded soldier was supported and slowly conducted to the front porch of the humble residence; and in response to Jim's gentle, timid rap at the front door, there appeared two white ladies.

They speechlessly gazed inquiringly at us, and seemed horror-stricken at the sight of the pale face and blood-besmeared clothing of a hatless soldier in blue, who opened the conversation with, "Ladies, I am an enemy, as my uniform indicates; but I am very badly wounded, and helpless." Before he could even commence to explain the cause of his presence and appearance, one of the ladies exclaimed, "Oh, you poor soul! you are welcome, thrice welcome, to our house, *whoever* you are; come in, sir, come in." The wounded "enemy," joyfully surprised at such an exhibition of kindness and sympathy, gladly staggered toward the door, when one of these kind ladies remarked:

"See! the poor fellow can scarcely stand; let's help him, sister, — take hold that side;" and the two ladies tenderly assisted Jim in supporting the fainting soldier into the house, and comfortably seating him before a grand old fire on the hearth.

MRS. HAMBRICK.

Would you know the name of the mistress of this humble residence, whose nobility of soul elevated her above sectional feeling, and whose large heart's generous impulses could not be halted before sectional prejudices, and whose sympathy for human suffering could neither be measured nor restrained by the *color* of a uniform? Her name is Mrs. Carrie E. Hambrick, a widow lady, who had fought the battles of life bravely and singlehanded for many years, and whose residence at present (May, 1880) is in the city of Atlanta, Georgia. The other lady, equally noble-hearted, was her sister, who was then temporarily sojourning with her.

"Now, tell us all about how you got hurt," said Mrs. Hambrick, kneeling beside the form drooping in the easy-chair, and gazing sympathetically into the ghastly features, her sister standing beside her; "please tell us all about it." With considerable difficulty the writer responded, "Well, ladies, I'm an escaped Union prisoner; was recaptured to-day by two armed men, — one in our uniform, — who took me into the woods over there, and gave me two minutes to pray; I ran, and they fired at me three or four times, and shot me through once, as you see. I know I'm badly wounded — perhaps mortally; I am growing weaker every moment, and can only hope to die in peace with you." The countenances of the two ladies were now bathed in tears. Suddenly Mrs. Hambrick's face was buried in her apron, and she sobbed aloud; then raising her noble face toward Jim, she inquired:

"And were you with him all the time?"

"Yes 'um, — I seed de whole thing, mum," She then vehemently exclaimed:

"Oh, the villains! Oh, the murderous, cowardly villains! Shame, shame on our folks!" Then turning to her sister, she said, "Sister, we heard the four shots; remember, I remarked it at the time?" The sister replied in the affirmative, adding, "Over in this direction" (pointing). Jim said, "Yes, 'um, dat's de place," and the writer nodded assent. "Well," said Mrs. H., arising and tenderly addressing the writer, "we must take off your coat, dress your wound, give you some warm supper, and put you to bed; we can't let you die with us, — you must *live*."

> "How softly on the bruised heart
> A word of kindness falls;
> And to the dry and parched soul
> The moistening tear-drop calls."

The blood-besmeared coat was carefully removed and the underclothing cut, exposing to view a ghastly, gaping wound, the sight of which brought forth fresh denunciations of the "contemptible, cowardly scoundrels," and an additional flow of sympathetic tears. The soldier looked at the ugly, bubbling wound through his breast, and, in spite of the tender encouragement of the ladies to the contrary, expressed his misgivings as to its effect. He knew that it was a bad wound, in a very dangerous place.

The two small children of Mrs. Hambrick, Isaac and Tallulah, — a sweet little girl, with bright eyes and sunny hair, — stood mutely by, gazing at the strange scene with childish simplicity, apparently horrified witnesses of the *bloody* work being performed by tender hearts and willing hands.

The wound was tenderly washed and dressed; warm water — soft cloths — sympathy — kind words and careful hands were brought into requisition for the purpose, but the "bathing" afforded by the tears of sympathetic souls seemed far more potent than all the rest to lift up the drooping spirits of the soldier, and encourage him to live. Then came warm bread and butter and hot coffee — royal luxuries. Foodless all day, and the experiences of it, had made the wounded stranger absolutely *ravenous;* hence the strange luxuries kindly placed before him disappeared almost instantly. The good ladies jocularly alluded to the "mysterious disappearance" as an encouraging sign of speedy recovery, and the soldier wonderfully revived.

"Now tell us who you are, and where's your home," said Mrs. H., cheerfully. The soldier's name, rank, and home were given; and his revival brought forth copious tears of gratitude, upon attempting to express his obligations for such unexpected kindness and sympathy. "Oh! never mind that," said Mrs. Hambrick, interrupting his rather awkward effort; "we would be only too glad to comfort *any one* in your pitiable condition." After Jim had also partaken freely of the luxurious "spread," the writer said to him, "Now, Jim, you shall have a chance to punish yourself for falling asleep. I'm going to send you to Atlanta. Will you go for me?" Jim promptly replied, "Suttainly; ob course I'll go." He was thereupon instructed how to be guided by the compass; to proceed north-westwardly, avoiding roads, until he reached the railroad east of Atlanta; then to move cautiously westward until hailed by Federal pickets. He was thoroughly posted as to the extreme danger of trifling with or hesitating before an *outpost;* and the writer, taking pains to particularize and simplify, explained: "Now, remember, Jim, when the picket yells '*Halt!*' you *stop* — don't move an inch; he will then ask, '*Who comes there?*' then you speak right out *immediately*, and say, '*A friend with the countersign;*' then he'll say, '*Advance, friend, with the countersign;*' then you walk right up to the picket, — *don't be afraid,* now, — and stand before his bayonet and tell him your story, and hand him this paper this lady has kindly written for us; now, will you do it, Jim, and be careful about it?"

"Suttain to do it — suttain!" (But will he?)

"One other thing, Jim: if you see the pickets are not

faced *this* way, look out! they're Confederates; circle away around them, as we've often done before."

Mrs. Hambrick had kindly written on a card the name, rank, and corps of the writer, together with her name and a description of the location of her residence, which she now handed to Jim, who received his final caution, bade us "good-night," and departed through the darkness on his perilous mission. The distance to Atlanta from this point is about ten and a half miles northwestward.

The good ladies then prepared the grand old featherbed which stood in a corner of the front-room, and announced that it was ready for the wounded stranger to occupy, and assisted him to its side. "White sheets! who ever heard of *white sheets?*" The stranger vigorously protested against *soiling* so grand a luxury. "Don't put me in there; my wound is bleeding yet," he urged, as he called attention to the dark blood which slowly oozed from the ghastly orifice, and rolled in thick drops down the body, "I'll not consent to soil your bed."

"Oh, you poor, dear soul!" exclaimed Mrs. H., as she forcibly pressed the helpless form down upon the snowy sheets, "what is my bed compared to your life and comfort? There! lie there, and not another word about it!" There was unwilling obedience, but in a few moments soothing relief came with deep slumber. How long the patient slept, he knows not; but when he awoke, during the still hours of the night, his eyes opened and beheld the motherly features of Mrs. Hambrick, whose form was leaning over the bedside, and whose eyes peered inquiringly into the pale features of the stranger. With low, sweet voice, full of tender sympathy, she inquired:

"How do you feel now, Lieutenant?"

"Better, I guess, dear lady, — slept sweetly. But what are you doing here, — why not retired?"

"Never mind me. Are you better, think you?"

"Yes, I feel much refreshed, — much better. I've been dreaming of one your kindness reminded me of, but who's gone, and I thought the distance between us very short. But you need rest; I can rest as well without care, so please go."

She did not reply, but continued that steady, inquiring look into the writer's face, as she slowly moved backward from the bedside. In a few moments he was again asleep. When he next awoke it was by the gentle pressure of a warm hand upon his forehead, and he slowly opened his eyes to look into the same anxious, smiling countenance. "What! you here yet?" he faintly asked. "Never mind me," said she; "do you want anything?"

"Nothing — nothing." She then gently leaned over the writer and earnestly spoke to him a few moments of *death* and *eternity* — the uncertainty of his recovery. She was informed by the latter that her views were in accord with his early education and the teachings of his mother, and that in the midst of his recent trials and sufferings, instead of dreading, he had actually *coveted* the change; and he felt even more grateful as he realized he was in the hands of Christian people. Again exhausted nature slept. Considerable time — he knows not how long — elapsed, when he was awakened still again by the suppressed murmur of voices beside him; the speakers were not aware that they had awakened the subject of their conversation. Said one, "I do hope he will last till the Federals come." "He appears to enjoy rest; I guess he'll feel stronger in the morning," whispered the other "Well," said the first, "we must do all we can." The ladies retired, and the writer thought, "Those tender-hearted ladies would have me worse than I really am." He soon again fell asleep, and slept until broad daylight of —

October 9. — It seems that the news of the presence of a wounded Federal officer had quickly spread about the neighborhood, together with rumors as to the cowardly manner in which the wound was given, for very early in the morning a number of ladies in the neighborhood visited Mrs. Hambrick, spoke sympathizingly to the "wounded Federal," and in strong language denounced the "cowardly brutes" who could thus attempt to murder the captured and helpless. Later, Mrs. Hambrick received a visit from a Confederate soldier, a Mr. Burdit, who rather unceremoniously and officiously entered the chamber with, "Heigh-ho! What you got here, eh? *Heard* you had a sick Yank over here." "No, Mr. Burdit, but wounded,—in a cowardly way, too,—a Federal officer, and he's quite low. Please be more quiet," obsequiously urged Mrs. Hambrick. "Yaas, I know'd he was a Yank by that blue coat thar," said he, as he carelessly inspected that bloody garment. Approaching the bedside, and seemingly peering rather impudently into the pale features of the wounded "enemy," he exclaimed, as he beheld the lustreless eyes fixed upon his dreaded butternut uniform, creating any thing but pleasant memories:

"Well, Yank,—see that?" (Holding up a shattered hand, well bandaged.) "I've just come from the *Wilderness*, where your man Grant got such a terrible flogging!"

"Indeed?" feebly responded the wounded man, rather indifferently.

"Maybe you don't believe me?"

"Yes, yes; only we probably differ as to what constitutes a 'flogging.'"

"Well, we'll both agree before we get through the fight as to what it is,—don't you reckon?"

"Oh, possibly."

"We're bound to whip the fight, you know,—no mistake about *that*. We're *bound* to whip the fight!—Eh?"

"I said nothing, sir. I'm in no condition to settle it by argument."

"Well, I'll just tell you, Yank, —" Mrs. Hambrick here kindly interposed with, —

"Now, Mr. Burdit, you must stop this; he's in no condition to argue with you, and you shall not taunt him in my house." (Noble woman!)

"Oh, I ain't a hurtin' on him, am I?"

"Well, you see, he's perfectly helpless, and you ought to be *ashamed* of yourself."

To the credit of "private Burdit" be it said, he then subsided in a very cheerful and gentlemanly manner, and was learning from Mrs. H. the circumstances of the wounding, when one of the children drove him unceremoniously to the woods by charging through the rear door with the excited exclamation, "The Federals are coming!" Glory hallelujah! At the writer's request the front-door was thrown wide open, and shortly after a body of eight or ten mounted Federal cavalrymen rode slowly by the house, with cocked carbines in their right hands, hardly looking to the right or left, but gazing intently down the road ahead of them, as they rode grandly and cautiously forward. "They're going by; they're going by!" exclaimed Mrs. Hambrick's little boy, Isaac. "That's the advance guard, as I live," joyfully exclaimed the wounded soldier, with a desperate effort to raise his head higher upon the pillow. With breathless anxiety we awaited the approach of the main force, which shortly after appeared, one hundred and fifty strong, escorting an ambulance and surgeon, and halted before the door. How the command "Halt!" rang out through the clear morning air. The next moment, a Federal sergeant leaped through the door to the bedside, with, "Ah! Lieutenant, we've come for you!" and almost immediately the room was filled with officers and soldiers of the command, faithful Jim in the midst of them. Veritable blue-coats at last; reaching our lines assured now; visions of home and friends The rescued soldier was so completely overcome with unbounded joy, that for some moments he was absolutely *speechless;* hot tears coursing down the pallid cheeks were the only evidences of inexpressible gratitude within.

"After long agony,
Rapture of bliss!"

Many moments of rare pleasure has the writer experienced during a life extending through thirty-eight years, embracing many of its charms and blessings, but to this particular moment, when the cheerful blue-coats swarmed into his presence, dispelling the gloomy clouds of dread suspense which surrounded him, and banishing fears and brightening hopes, does he accord the no small honor of affording him the most complete satisfaction and unalloyed joy of any moment in his life. This force was of the New York cavalry command of Gen. Garrard, and commanded by a captain, a noble officer, whose name the writer greatly regrets he forgot, and who, with the surgeon, approached the bedside and carefully examined the ugly wound through the breast. "It's a very bad wound," said the surgeon; and inquired, "Did you spit blood?" The writer replied in the affirmative, and the surgeon nodded, and whispered significantly to the captain.

The writer was now assisted by numerous willing hands to partially dress, and was bundled up comfortably by the ladies for the rugged voyage, and numerous strong arms of the "boys in blue" gladly bore his weakened form to the comfortable ambulance awaiting him at the gate. Here the ladies, who had followed with encouraging words and small articles of comfort, again burst into tears. The wounded but happy soldier recited as best he could the many acts of kindness and sacrifices of these noble ladies, and was overjoyed as he listened to the glowing compliments and warm thanks tendered to them, over and over again, by our gallant officers and soldiers. At parting, the captain commanding grew eloquent in a short, touching speech, promising remembrance, and warmly tendering the thanks of himself and command "for your great kindness, ladies, and sacrifices made for an unfortunate one of our number." Jim, now *completely* forgiven, was placed in the ambulance to support his wounded companion. The ladies each stepped upon the rear step of the ambulance, and implanted farewell kisses upon bloodless lips, enjoining earnestly, "Now, write to us if you ever get well." They were assured by a feeble voice the great pleasure such an opportunity would afford. The final "good-day, ladies," was numerously spoken; there was a general polite lifting of blue caps, and the column slowly moved toward the long-coveted Federal lines.

Supported by the strong arms of Jim, the rescued soldier leaned outward to obtain a last, lingering look at the receding forms of two of the noblest of women, and painfully realized his utter inability to fully appreciate their nobility of soul, and the deep, warm sympathy for a suffering "enemy" whom a cowardly, hostile bullet had suddenly pressed to the very verge of eternity; and without their tender care to comfort him, and their kind, cheering words of *hope*, tenderly urged in upon the soul that had well-nigh taken its flight, the dim flame would have long since been extinguished, and this volume would not be written to record the evidences of their nobility, outranking all titles bestowed by human hands!

There were now brought to the rear of the ambulance, for the writer's inspection, three Confederate pickets who had been captured *en route*. One of the captors asked, "Do these look like those fellows, Lieutenant, — anything like 'em at all?" The writer looked steadily at the trio of captives in Confederate uniforms, and how *imploringly* did they look at him! With breathless anxiety, and meek and humble countenances did they await his response, and seemed to breathe freer as he slowly shook his head with, "No, none of these. Where were these taken?"

"We were on picket duty, sir," quickly and timidly responded one of them.

"They disputed our passage to you, and we run 'em down and *gobbled* 'em," said one of our boys.

"They're *soldiers*, taken in the line of *duty*, and ought not to be harmed. I don't want them harmed on my account," earnestly responded the writer, and the poor fellows looked up gratefully into the ambulance.

"Well, it's a d—d lucky thing for you fellows that you don't look like the d—d cowardly scoundrels!" said one of the boys in blue to the relieved captives. "There's too much of this thing going on, and only one in a thousand gets away to tell of it."

"And it's about time there was some mustering out done on the other side," added another.

"Yes, and the sooner we commence at it the better," chimed in another, with a suspicious side-glance at the timid captives marching through the dust behind the ambulance, who seemed well aware that the threatening remarks were intended for their ears.

The writer peered inquiringly at one of the sergeants, who participated in the conversation, who, in response, brought his horse up near the ambulance, only to hear repeated, —

"I don't want these prisoners harmed on my account, sergeant."

"That's all right," replied he; "the boys 're just scaring 'em a little, that's all; it'll do 'em good."

We had proceeded about a quarter of a mile from Mrs. Hambrick's, when, incredible as it may seem, a solitary shot was fired at our column from the edge of the timber, about three hundred yards from the road, and a single bullet passed over it with the old familiar hissing sound. "Bushwhackers!" shouted several of our boys at once. The fence beside the road was razed in a twinkle, and a half dozen blue-coats dashed across the open intervening field in the direction of the lingering smoke of the rifle.

The column halted for the result. The chase was a short, fruitless one, and when the pursuers returned, the captain rode to the ambulance and inquired, —

"Lieutenant, how were your friends dressed?"

After being informed, he continued: "These fellows answered that description, — one in butternut and one in blue; we got a sight of 'em, but the scoundrels ran into a swamp and escaped us; wish we'd caught 'em for you." This supposition corresponds with the information afterwards acquired, to the effect that the next morning after the shooting, Fowler, with Singleton, was trailing the writer with hounds; that his name had unwittingly been mentioned in the presence of the writer, and, fearing disagreeable consequences, he had "determined to finish his intended victim, at any risk." (You didn't get up quite early enough, "brother" Fowler.)

A word or two more to these chivalrous gentlemen: —

Let me state to you, brother Fowler, brother Singleton, that, had you been caught on that occasion, you may safely "reckon" that neither of you would have experienced the delight of perusing in this volume the eulogistic references made by the *facts* to your prowess, chivalry, manhood, and — marksmanship.

Our little column passed through Decatur, and another little jaunt of six miles brought us to Atlanta. Atlanta! that "Hood had made up his mind to hold at all hazards." Atlanta! that "the Yankees can never take, sir." Atlanta! before whose gates the rescued soldier, while concealed in distant Southern forests, had so often heard the thunder of Federal cannon. Atlanta! at peace beneath the flag of the stripes and stars. As we neared the fortifications, the escorted ambulance passed the battle-field of July 22d, and over the very road beside which its wounded occupant was captured, which spot was immediately identified with much interest; but the grand feast to his bedimmed vision was the sight of the *old flag*. How majestically it floated where before he had seen only "stars and bars." Never before did the flag of the Union appear so bright and glorious; never was he prouder of the uniform he wore; never so desirous of witnessing a vigorous prosecution of the war for the Union; never before so appreciative — so delighted — so comfortable — so safe — so satisfied under the glorious old stars and stripes.

> "Then up with our banner bright,
> Sprinkled with starry light,
> Spread the fair emblem from mountain to shore,
> And through the sounding sky,
> Loud let the Nation cry,
> *Union and Liberty, one evermore!*"

Failure to readily find the hospital of the Fifteenth Army Corps resulted in the wounded soldier's reception into the general hospital of the Army of the Cumberland. The news of his misfortune and rescue soon spread in the immediate vicinity, and he at once became an unenvied object of curiosity. Soldiers and citizens and hospital *attachés* assembled in and about the large hospital-tent, gazing curiously at the annoyed and suffering new-comer, and eagerly soliciting information concerning his experiences; visitors, nurses, and surgeons asked innumerable questions, wise and *otherwise*, which greatly annoyed the unfortunate fortunate, who was wearied after the long ride, and of all things most desired rest. The surgeon-in-chief soon entered, and elbowed his way to the side of the tortured new patient; asked a few hurried questions; looked seriously at the gaping wound, from which the dark, thick blood again began to slowly ooze; learned of the long, tedious ride; recognized the meaning of the woe-begone appearance of his new patient, and immediately ordered the curious crowd from the tent, and instructed the kind soldier-nurse to permit no person whatever to converse with the object of their curiosity. The writer of course felt greatly relieved, and was just relapsing into sweet slumber, when he was disturbed by the appearance of three or four surgeons with the nurse, who announced to his unwilling ears that they had come to take a diagnosis of the wound, and to see it properly attended to and dressed. The ordeal, though very painful, was cheerfully endured, and the delicate duties of the surgeons tenderly performed, during which the remarks were made: "Just missed the subclavian artery," one kindly said to the patient, smilingly; "an eighth of an inch higher, my boy, would have settled it." Another said, "The ball passed just below where the subclavian and axillary arteries join." All seemed to concur in such declarations as, "mighty narrow escape;" "close call;" "ugly wound," "bad place;" "the d—d cowardly villains;" etc., etc. The kind torturers, occasionally, tenderly made inquiries of the patient, in response to which he informed them that during the evening of the shooting, and while at the house of the noble lady, when he drew breath the wound bubbled, and he frequently spat blood. All concurred that the ball had penetrated the upper lobe of the right lung. The surgeons stood aside, indulging in private conference concerning the "new case;" after which the surgeon in charge of the hospital-tent alone returned, gave the nurse instructions concerning treatment, diet, etc., and passed on his rounds to the bedsides of other unfortunates. In the excitement and confusion attending the too warm "reception" at the hospital, Jim became separated from the writer, and in obedience to the surgeon's orders was probably included in the ejected crowd of curious spectators, and the most strenuous efforts to ascertain his whereabouts failed; nor has the writer seen or heard of him since, excepting the indirect information that he remained with Garrard's cavalry in the capacity of a servant. Should this volume and the writer's location ever come to his knowledge, beyond a doubt he will bear willing testimony as to the scenes and incidents occurring in the woods as herein related; and he may accept this as a certificate of full and complete pardon for falling asleep while on "guard duty," and always be assured that his old companion of sylvan retreats will at any time be more than rejoiced to cordially greet and welcome him. Despite the precious privilege of communicating with home and friends, after two and a half months of unaccounted-for absence, and the tenderest possible care, and the glorious consolation of being safe among friends and beneath the protecting folds of our flag of the stripes and stars, and happy, —

despite all these, the exciting incidents of the recent past, and the great loss of blood, produced their evil effects. The patient rapidly sank, and for two days remained in a state of half-consciousness, the spirit seeming to linger hesitatingly upon that indistinct border where faint life gradually fades into — dissolution.

As soon as possible, the writer was removed from the tent to more comfortable quarters, within a residence which had been appropriated for hospital purposes, and where he had been "booked" for removal and classed among the "severe cases." This was on —

October 12. — Thence followed more than a week of careful, tender care, and feverish tossings of the bed-ridden patient, except when forced under the quiet and dreamy influence of — morphine. Letters were dictated, and communications attempted with friends in the far North. The only exercise permitted was that necessitated by the morning and evening dressing of the painful wound; 'twas not the wound that pained so much, but dreadful, constant pains seemed to shoot spasmodically the entire length of the right arm, and to linger continually in the shoulder, elbow, and joints of the wrist and hand. Almost daily was the patient compelled to submit to the *delightful* process of burning off proud flesh with caustic from the surroundings of the wound, and experience the *soothing* sensation produced by streams of tepid water forced entirely through the body, to keep the wound "sweet" and "healthy."

Upon earnest inquiry, the patient was informed that his division, and the whole Fifteenth Corps, was back between Atlanta and Chattanooga looking after the rebs, who had all gone north in the endeavor to flank Sherman out of Atlanta; which the boys all seemed to consider a "good joke." We occasionally heard of the battles in the *rear;* and the writer, being the only member of the Fifteenth Corps in the room, took great pride in listening to, and exulting over, the reports of the gallant conduct of detachments of his old corps in contact with superior numbers of the enemy. Prominent among these events was the attempt of Maj. Gen. French, C. S. A., on October 5, to carry by *storm* our works at Altoona, Georgia, and who sent to Brig. Gen. Corse, commanding that post, the startling announcement that he was "entirely surrounded," and demanding immediate and "unconditional surrender," allowing *five minutes* to decide, "to avoid the needless effusion of blood," and patronizingly promising "most honorable treatment as prisoners of war."

The worthy and gallant representative of the old corps immediately replied, spurning the demand, "We are prepared for the needless effusion of blood, whenever it is agreeable to you." Notwithstanding the furious, bloody assault from surrounding and overwhelming forces which followed, the dauntless commander of the Fourth Division and his plucky soldiers tenaciously carried out the determination, against all comers, to "hold the fort."

Of *Corse* they did; and yet it was no more than was *expected* of a detachment of the old Fifteenth Corps.

Not relishing the terrible, bloody repulse resulting from actual encounter with such *stuff*, and realizing with horror "the needless effusion of blood" before the Federal works at Altoona, Gen. John B. Hood, commanding the entire Confederate army about Northern Georgia, on October 12 tested another small detachment of this old corps, — the Second Brigade of the Third Division, — placed within and *expected* to hold the fortifications at Resaca, Georgia. By the intimidation or buncombe process, he vainly sought to force to surrender a comparative "handful" of the same "stuff" which the bloody sting inflicted at Altoona admonished him not to assault. The "general commanding" sent the peremptory demand to the Union colonel, Clark R. Weaver, with the startling announcement that, "if the place is carried by assault, no prisoners will be taken!" While rather surprised at such a message from the "commander-in-chief" of overwhelming numbers, he promptly responded: "In my opinion, I can hold this post. If you want it, come and take it!"

The test seemed to satisfy the "commanding general" that the same sort of indomitable pluck which had cost him so much to discover at Altoona, would be also found, unadulterated, in the fearless little brigade expected to defend Resaca. The remaining test of assault was wisely waived.

Some two months later, Gen. Sherman selected the Second Division of the same old corps, upon the staff of which the proud writer belonged, to assault and carry by storm the important stronghold and final "link" that connected him with the sea, — Fort McAllister, below Savannah, Georgia, — which was grandly done, despite planted torpedoes, *chevaux-de-frise*, artillery and musketry fire, and the entire garrison killed or captured. "To secure this important remaining 'link,'" Gen. Sherman stated, "I trusted entirely to this division of infantry, — the Second of the Fifteenth Corps, — the same old division that I had commanded at Shiloh and Vicksburg, and in which I felt a special pride and confidence."

The brother sufferers of the writer in the double room of the residence hospital deserve passing notice. Among the wounded soldiers, comparatively insignificant incidents were greedily seized upon, if the slightest opportunity was afforded by them to create mirth or laughter, and all sorts of jests and stories were told to cheer the weary hours. Personal peculiarities were made the subject of humorous comments, and the quaint expressions of faithful soldier-nurses furnished ample opportunity to test the powers of mimicry. Thus through the lengthened hours of suffering ran a silver thread of merriment, which rendered even painful existence agreeable, and the quaint jokes, fantastic performances, odd innuendoes, cant expressions, and caustic wit sparkled in relief of the dull drag of time, and provoked begrudged smiles on pallid countenances in spite of intense suffering. The writer, then unable to write, cheerfully accepted the proffered services of Capt. Morse, on the "sick, lame, and lazy" list, who kindly volunteered to fill out the writer's diary, and the following is presented as the record of the unrelenting critic: —

"*October 12 to 23.* — Still at hospital, Army of the Cumberland. Inmates of our room are, —

Chaplain C. — Incomprehensible; decidedly orthodox; always managing to save from dinner enough beef for supper; is sick, be it remembered, not wounded; chief pet of the nurses; when awake, is generally growling; universally beloved (over the left).

Lieut. Seltzer. — No relation to the *water* of the same name; awaiting leave of absence. Not wounded, but has been very sick.

Lieut. Craven. — Recovering rapidly; very accommodating, and cheerfully aiding those around him who are less able to aid themselves than he. A friend in need and indeed.

Lieut. S., Adjutant —— Ohio Infantry. — Wounded through the leg, but rapidly recovering, and entertains great fear that he will be able to "navigate" without the aid of crutches before his leave of absence arrives; wants to go home on crutches to gain more sympathy. (Surmise.)

Capt. B., One Hundred and Twenty-fourth Ohio Infantry. — Fatherly and kind at times, but his bad wound forces the fact that he is apt to be a little excusably surly at all times.

Lieut. K. — (We dubbed him "Shanks.") Magnus ego! Wounded; disabled encyclopædia! Great know-all, — know nothing; better never attempt to argue, especially on the subject of religion; he knows it all, every bit. Jack enough to think equal numbers of cavalry far superior to infantry! What an ——.

Capt. Ream, Eighty-sixth Indiana Infantry.— Wounded at Kenesaw Mountain through the hand (minie-ball). The very life and joy of the room; enjoyed by all; jolly and cheerful all the days; very obliging and attentive to those who "caught it" at the front worse than himself; has taken a great interest in the owner of this diary, and waits upon him and reads to him faithfully, as well as keeps him cheerful and happy.

Chaplain Van Valkenburg. — "Sweet, melodious voice — always sent for, when at home, to sing at camp-meetings." Boasts inordinately of his home, — "splendid wife and family." Extraordinarily fond of fresh milk, and takes great comfort in frequently announcing that he's "going to board with a cow." Good, honest, plain gentleman.

Capt. Paisley and Lieut. Lord. — Both very sick; too ill to be about or leave their cots, and too weak to exhibit personal peculiarities.

Lieut. Bailey, of the Second Division Staff, Fifteenth Corps. — Astray in our "Cumberland" hospital, but his corps hospital is miles away, and his corps is rattling old Hood between here and Chattanooga; takes great pride in that Fifteenth Corps — "old corps of Grant and Sherman;" Twentieth Corps nowhere in comparison; has been very low indeed, but don't know it, — too low to make much noise, or to laugh loudly, but hugely enjoys the witticisms and jokes perpetrated by those around him; bears an ugly wound, — narrow escape; is alone in his opinion that he is able to travel to St. Louis. We hope he will be strong enough in a few weeks. Last, but not least, is —

G., of the Engineer Corps. — A long, lean, cadaverous, glassy-eyed, selfish, avaricious fellow, caring entirely for self. Not wounded, — of course not; continually growling at something or somebody, and actually knowing more than all the others combined; always uneasy, — never satisfied; not sound in the head; monopolizing every thing, owning every thing, knowing every thing; never warm; the friend of "niggers" generally; nurses never doing any thing right; every thing goes wrong; says he's married; must be perpetually diseased, and a very unhandy thing to have about a house or in a family, and makes his wife the sympathized being of all who know her husband. G., *adieu.*

Capt. Morse, Twentieth Connecticut Infantry, Twentieth Army Corps. — Not very sick, — not very well; fond of billiards; not fond of hospital or sickness; a free and easy kind of a fellow, bound to take the world easy."

But it must be remembered that the volunteer whose pen and ideas were placed at the service of the disabled patient admits he was " not very sick, and not very well," hence in excellent condition to be sorely annoyed and vexed by the "growling and grumbling" of those in much worse condition than himself. Men who are bedridden and suffering hour after hour, day after day, are not expected to evince the most amiable dispositions; neither is it surprising that convalescence should create exuberance of spirits at the prospect of meeting friends at home, which would find vent in frequent "slopping over" in unguarded references to anticipated bliss.

It was the sixth or seventh day after being shot that the patient's hope was clouded by the kind surgeon informing him seriously of the great danger of secondary hemorrhage. After considerately and delicately preparing the way, he said: "We lose a good many that way, and it occurs before or about the tenth day. I have dreaded all along to tell you, but I consider it a solemn duty, now the time approaches, to do so, and to further say that if it *does* occur in your case, I see no way of saving you." The desponding patient inquired, —

"And do you think it will occur?"

"I'm very much afraid of it, and have been expecting it; still, there's a hope, a slight hope, but I'm sorry I cannot give you much encouragement."

The patient was sad and pensive, the surgeon continuing: "If you've any matters to attend to at home, I advise you to do so at once; for if it *does* occur, you'll have but a few moments. You see, from the nature of the wound it will be internal, and we can't control it or reach it, — *that's* the trouble."

The patient's drooping spirits were not revived by the surgeon's faint attempt to encourage him by urging; "There is a chance in remaining perfectly quiet until the tenth day passes."

The surgeon departed, but his words had created dark gloom and despondency in the patient's mind. Bright hope dispelled by a cloud of gloom! Silent thoughts; gloomy forebodings; suspense; cheerfulness fled; sleep almost impossible.

> "A grief without a pang, — void, dark, and drear,
> A stifled, drowsy, unimpassioned grief,
> Which finds no natural outlet, no relief,
> In word, or sigh, or tear."

The ominous "tenth day" approached, — arrived, —

and, after torturing the patient with the agony of *suspense*, gradually faded away like its predecessors; sweet hope brightening and beaming as its shadows deepened into the night, — safe.

"Not yet, my boy," said the surgeon with sympathy beaming in his countenance, reflecting the brightening hope in the pale features beside him, — " not yet; wait until to-morrow morning, and then I'll say you're out of danger."

Morning came, and very early the kind, interested surgeon was at the bedside, with warm congratulations. Later, congratulations came from wounded comrades in the room, and new hope brought new life and strength. Hood's destruction of the line of communication with the North, which prevented the approach of friends to Atlanta, did not deter the wounded, who were able, from being safely transferred to the rear. Notwithstanding the wise refusal of the surgeon of the Army of the Cumberland to indorse or encourage the attempt to obtain leave of absence by daily appearance with helpless right arm in a board sling, and persistent personal application at the "Headquarters, Army of the Tennessee," in Atlanta, the patient did obtain such leave in the latter part of October, and under the fatherly care of Capt. Ream, Eighty-sixth Indiana Infantry, started North in a baggage-car, by rail. The car was full of Union wounded; those who "caught it" severely being attended by those who "caught it" slightly.

There was a break of only four miles in the railroad, and the intense desire to reach home and the comforts of civilization was sufficient to overrule the protest of the surgeon, which the patient vainly attempted to treat as a jest by replying, —

"Your advice would be good for the Army of the Cumberland, doctor; but folks expect more of the Army of the Tennessee boys." "Well," said the good-natured surgeon, smiling, yet talking earnestly, "remember one thing, Lieutenant: I don't take the responsibility, and I hate to have you go." As the train of baggage-cars filled with wounded slowly moved away, he said to the "slightly wounded" Capt. Ream concerning his "severely wounded" *protégé*, "Take good care of him, Captain." The promise was cheerfully given, and more than faithfully fulfilled. The inordinate laughter caused by his excellent humor and flow of wit precluded the possibility of gloom, and tended, for the time, to subdue pain; and even if ample *compensation* followed, the mirth was worth the cost. We rested overnight at the southern end of the break, in order to undertake the "four miles" over a rough, hilly road in a springless lumber-box wagon, starting afresh the next morning. The "head-quarters" of the wounded "army" were on the plantation of a wealthy, corpulent old planter, whose name was not preserved for this volume. The wounded occupied all the spare rooms and porches of the buildings, and the proprietor seemed as cheerful and jolly as any of the company. During the sultry Indian summer evening an incident occurred which will serve to illustrate how slight invitations were promptly accepted and small opportunities eagerly seized upon by wounded soldiers homeward bound, to create mirth or amusement. Capt. Ream, with his "choir" (save the mark!), stood in the front yard, and rivalling the other voices of the night, sang, melodiously (?) —

> "Old John Brown, he's dead and gone;
> We ne'er shall see him more.
> He used to wear an old gray coat,
> All buttoned down before."

The old planter proprietor approached and patronizingly inquired of the humorous captain, —

"What do you call that? My stars, gemmen, that's a right purty tune!"

"Did you never hear that before, sir?" asked Ream.

"No, 'pon honah. Ain't thar no mo' varses?"

"Yes, lots more verses; we'll give you another one."

The verse was repeated. The corpulent old gent leaned upon his stout cane, his head slightly turned to one side, and when finished he said, "Now that is fine, sir, fine; better'n t'other varse." "But the next verse is still better — more expression in it," said Ream, looking sedately at the old planter and casting a roguish glance at his wounded charge, seated near by and enjoying the "performance." "Then, sir, by all that's good, let's have it, sir," said the old planter.

The original verse was again repeated.

The apparently half-suspecting listener bowed his head and exclaimed, —

"Gemmen, that sounds just like the fust varse for all the world." "No, no," quickly retorted Ream; "the music is the same, — the music confuses you a little, that's all." "Yes 'twas, sir," persisted the corpulent gent. "Now, you just sing that *same varse* over agin, an' see?"

"Oh, we can't repeat, sir," replied Ream; "on account of the extreme length of the programme, there can be no repetition, — too many verses, — and there's the *chorus*. You haven't heard the chorus yet, sir."

"Well, sir, I'd like it, I know, — sing that ar."

The original was again repeated.

The corpulent old planter straightened up, with a broad, knowing smile upon his rugged countenance, brought the end of his cane suddenly down, exclaiming, "Storm my buttons, gemmen, if that ain't the same thing, right over and over!" and he hobbled toward his porch, laughing heartily, and informing those he met that "them fellers, sir, are singing the *same* thing, right over and over, as I'm a sinner;" while the "choir" and "audience" joined in peals of laughter until the portly form had retreated from sight. The jaunt over the four miles of break was a terrible ordeal for the writer; thence speedily to Chattanooga and to Nashville, where the wisdom of the surgeon at Atlanta was demonstrated. The relapse came, and the writer was ordered and taken to the officers' hospital, while his comrades proceeded homeward. While here, he received many kind attentions and delicacies at the hands of Mr. H. B. Blood, of St. Louis, of the Western Sanitary Commission.

To add, if possible, to the danger and suffering, through the carelessness of *somebody* a serious mistake was made in administering the wrong medicine. Result: delirium, which continued, under repeated doses, during a whole night, when the nurse, alarmed at the effects, summoned the surgeon, whom he would not disturb during the night, who at once discovered and rectified the mistake, and expressed surprise that results were no worse. The writer was informed that during the night his "audience" — no small one — was entertained by various military commands: orders to "charge, — lie down, — aim low, — load and fire at will, — bring up that ammunition, — hurry forward that battery, — shoot the cowardly guerillas down," etc. But the person who had unwittingly furnished this rare "amusement" was only conscious, in the morning, of utter exhaustion, and of the dreaded fact that his wound had recommenced bleeding freely. Over a week he lay helpless, when, under kind care and careful treatment, he rallied, and on the eighth day of November (one month after the dialogue in the woods) he was again speeding, with other wounded Federals and some Confederates, on a comfortable hospital-car between Nashville and Louisville, in charge of a special nurse, homeward-bound.

On a bloody cot beside the writer lay a wounded Confederate, with ghastly countenance and lustreless eyes, who informed his Union companion that his leg had been amputated "close up." Beneath the cots on both sides of the car, soiled uniforms of blue and gray commingled in peace, and the proud eagle of the United States of America condescends to affiliation with the plain, ungraceful pelican of Louisiana, as brass buttons and equipments jingle together in harmonious contact.

November 9. — One month after the entry into Atlanta, the writer experienced the great delight of reaching his home in St. Louis, and receiving the congratulations and welcome accorded by relatives and friends, some of whom had been deterred from visiting Nashville by daily expectation of the present event; but the "reception" proved too much for exhausted nature, which demanded dear "compensation" in the shape of a second dreaded relapse. The government authorities peremptorily ordered the patient from his "headquarters," indiscreetly selected at the Lindell Hotel, to the quiet retreat of the officer's hospital at Jefferson Barracks, Missouri, situated on a beautiful site on the west bank of the Mississippi, twelve miles below the city, and overlooking the "Father of Waters." A careful diagnosis of the wound there resulted in the physician's opinion that, on account of the fatigue of the trip, mistreatment at the hospital at Nashville, excitement upon reaching home, and the enfeebled condition of the patient, it would probably prove fatal; and the patient's relatives were informed by the "surgeon-in-charge," Dr. Allen, that he saw "no hope of his ever returning to St. Louis." But in spite of evil predictions, and under excellent treatment, aided by delicious quiet and forced rest under the soothing, dreamy influence of morphine, the patient gradually grew convalescent; but it was nearly six months after that the wound ceased to suppurate, and small splinters of rib and scapula ceased occasionally to be forced out. In the early spring of 1865 the writer was able, with helpless right arm laced in a board sling, to visit St. Louis and other places, on short trips or "leaves;" and on one of these occasions the writer was handed by Missouri's war governor, Thomas C. Fletcher, in person, a mysterious envelope, with the cheerful remark, —

"It gives me great pleasure, *Captain*, to present you with this, upon the earnest request and recommendation of the colonel of your regiment."

The envelope contained a commission as captain of the writer's old company in the Sixth Missouri Infantry.

The formation of a disagreeable abscess near the healing wound; the inconvenience and annoyance of submitting to the process of "washing and dressing" twice each day, and of carrying about a cumbersome board sling to accommodate an almost paralyzed limb for half a year; the very painful gradual exercises necessary to recover partial use of the member that had borne the "brunt;" the pains and aches which had never ceased to predict coming storms (costly barometer!) or to follow ordinary use; and the pain now produced by the attempt to complete the manuscript for this volume, will constitute the concluding reference to the list of dangers and misfortunes which were entailed by the little leaden messenger which sped with cruel accuracy from the rifle in the woods. The list will serve to amply illustrate what has been amply demonstrated: that danger to life does not vanish before an entry on the muster-roll of the hopeful word "wounded."

The patient retained his "headquarters" at this hospital, the recipient of numerous favors and delicacies from relatives and friends, until after the surrender of Lee and Johnston; when the government, in recognition of the fact that it would no longer require the services, in any event, of its *disabled* soldiers, granted them, and among them the writer, honorable discharge from further service.

> "Never again call 'comrade'
> To the men who were comrades for years;
> Never to hear the bugles,
> Thrilling, sweet, and solemn;
> Never again call 'brother'
> To the men I think of with tears;
> Never again to ride or march
> In the dust of the marching column."

The day when we received the *last* report that Richmond was taken, an incident occurred at the barracks worthy of mention. Upon receipt of the "glorious news," the dark storm-clouds which had hovered over the earth began to clear away, and as they were rolled together and pushed by the western breeze away in the eastern sky, golden sunlight streamed from the western horizon, and painted in bold relief against the massive bank of retreating clouds a suggestive *bow of peace*, with a brilliancy and clearness seldom witnessed. It formed a complete shining arch over the barracks flagpole, from which fluttered the "storm-flag" of the garrison, its colors washed brighter by the storm, lit up with new beauty by the sunlight, and rendered still more glorious in contrast with the gloom beyond it. How typical of the situation! War-clouds, dark and dismal, retreating before the sunlight of peace! The *old flag* straightens in the breeze as if conscious of its triumph, and descending pearly mist furnishes the *coup-de-grace* to a scene of exquisite beauty.

> "Honor to thee, flag of the free,
> Emblem of sweet Liberty!"

With the restoration of peace came the restoration of communications between the North and South. The promise of October 8, 1864, was remembered and eagerly fulfilled. A note was directed to Mrs. Hambrick, at Decatur, Georgia, — another, — another which was promptly responded to by Mrs. H., and a long and interesting correspondence followed. Communications were also promptly established between the writer and the Freemans, and indirectly with old Aunt Mary. Numerous missives and photographs fluttered between the delighted correspondents, all in care of "Uncle Sam," and the writer's Georgia friends seemed overjoyed to learn of his escape, and that he was still alive. Mrs. Hambrick had frequently inquired of soldiers of Garrard's cavalry as to the condition of the writer, and had been considerably confused by conflicting reports. Her sister, she wrote, would not be satisfied that he reached Atlanta alive, until the receipt of his first letter from St. Louis. So incredulous was she, that, after the Federals had left Atlanta on the "march to the sea," she drove to the Federal burying-ground near that city, and spent the day in diligent search for the name of the writer, which she felt confident she would find ornamenting a crude head-board.

The writer has ample evidence completely identifying Fowler and Singleton. He knows their full names, places of residence, occupations, and standing, and would willingly give them to the public if he was not bound in honor to withhold the information. The writer has trustworthy information that Singleton, being pressed, admitted the whole affair, implicated Fowler, and corroborated the statement made by the writer to Mrs. Hambrick; that he pleaded, apart, with Fowler, during the conference in the woods, to spare the captive's life, but that Fowler was unyielding, and determined to shoot the captive, "because he had found out his name, and if he escaped to tell it, the Yankees would kill him and burn his house!" Singleton seemed to regard the affair as a good joke: that they "took a Yankee and a 'nigger' into the woods to kill them, and let 'em both get away." Singleton also admitted that he wore blue clothing. The writer has also what he considers ample evidence to the effect that Fowler was frequently interviewed by friends of the writer, but fear restrained confession; that Fowler protested his innocence, but threatened that "if any man or woman brought him into the scrape, he'd make 'em smoke." On another occasion, he threatened that "if any man or woman reported him to a Yankee, he would leave friends enough behind to see that he or she paid the forfeit of their lives for it." On another occasion, he announced that "whoever reported him would be punished with death." Upon being confronted, on another occasion, with the admission of Singleton implicating him, he replied,—

"Ah, just let him go on; but if any one has me taken up, and troubled about it, I have friends left behind, here, that will wreak vengeance in blood." On another occasion, during a discussion concerning the "affair," he was asked his opinion of such conduct, and " he declared he thought it no sin, — that God took no cognizance of any acts done in time of war."

To add insult to injury, it was diligently circulated in Mrs. Hambrick's neighborhood, and that lady was solemnly assured, shortly after the shooting, that the Yankee officer she had harbored was one who had escaped from Andersonville prison-pen, — a wild, daring, reckless desperado, a heartless, dissipated, and profane villain, who had been "prowling about within the Confederate lines, committing all manner of depredations too horrible to repeat;" and he also enjoyed the unenviable reputation of being "that formidable dare-devil scout in Sherman's army, widely known as 'Devil Jim'" (whoever he may be). It is not necessary to modestly quote the glowing accounts of how the "patent falsehoods" were promptly refuted, nor is it difficult to opine whence they came. It is sufficient that the infamous falsehoods, manifestly adduced as a counter-irritant, failed of their object.

"Fowler" having denied participation in the affair, the writer took steps to satisfy himself, beyond a doubt, of his guilt or innocence. It is not deemed necessary to lengthen the details of this undertaking, nor to disclose either the friends or the artist who were instrumental in executing the writer's purpose; suffice it to state, that in due time the writer became possessed of an excellent "picture," which he instantly recognized as that of the person who recaptured him in the woods and who told him his name was "Foster," but whose "comrade" unwittingly addressed as "Fowler," and from which the wood-cut in this volume was obtained.

In 1866, the "situation" in the neighborhood of Mrs. Hambrick was such that she was solemnly warned, and felt insecure in her person and home by reason of her well-known correspondence with the object of her kind care and solicitude in 1864; and at her suggestion, letters were addressed to her at Atlanta. It was also deemed advisable to resort to a ruse to insure to her peace of mind, and protection from secret threats or possible injury or damage. Accordingly, a letter was directed to her at Decatur, in the fine handwriting of a lady friend, Miss Susie A. Williams, then of St. Louis, purporting to be from the "sister" of the writer, informing her of the death of the writer from the effects of his wound, and thanking her for her great kindness to him. Another was forwarded by Judge James K. Knight, also then of St. Louis, to the same effect. The writer was then a law student in the latter's office. These "sad" missives, bordered with *deep mourning* were duly exhibited to the " proper parties " and to their " suspected friends," who seemed more at ease upon receipt of the "truly sad" intelligence, and Mrs. Hambrick's misgivings vanished upon the cessation of significant inquiries, coupled with gratuitous observations and taunts, and she enjoyed a long season of a feeling of perfect security, while through the Atlanta post-office, ten and a half miles away, there was maintained continually an interesting correspondence with the "deceased," who received his letters from Atlanta under the name of "Jno. Patton, Esq." This ruse was successfully maintained for a period of about *fourteen years*, and the paramount desire and determination not to endanger the personal security, welfare, or peace of mind of Mrs. Hambrick on any account, furnishes ample explanation of the withholding of this volume from earlier publication. The lady now resides in Atlanta; the reason of the withholding is by herself considered no longer extant, and the long-withheld "secret" is consequently spread broadcast. Through the perusal of this volume, undoubtedly, will the "interested parties" be first apprised of the "blissful ignorance" with which they have been blessed, and in which they have slumbered for the past fourteen years, and for which they ought to thank Mrs. Hambrick; but the surprise may also bring relief to guilty souls, through the consoling influences and operation of the Statute of Limitations.

In 1868, the writer had occasion to transact legal business with one of the most eminent statesmen and the greatest soldier of the age, Gen. Grant, who was then at the "Dent residence" on the old Gravois Road, a few miles west of St. Louis. The writer was cordially welcomed by the late commander of the old army to which he had belonged, and after the transaction of business, the General said, —

"So you were in the old Army of the Tennessee. That was a grand army; I'm always glad to meet a soldier of that army. By the way, what has the Convention done?" (Referring to the Democratic Convention of 1868, who had on that very day nominated his political opponent for the presidency.)

"They have nominated your opponent, General."

"Have they?" said he, quickly. "I haven't heard of it; who did they nominate?"

"Will you guess, General?"

"Well, I guess Hendricks."

"No."

"Hancock?"

"No."

"Well, I don't know who to guess, now."

"Seymour."

"What! Seymour? And who for vice-president?"

"Frank Blair."

The hero of Appomattox looked out upon the storm which was raging, as the two sat upon the broad porch, suddenly bit a piece from the end of his cigar, and turning squarely toward the writer, said:—

"Well, the *soldiers* will not vote for Seymour;" and gazing thoughtfully at the rain-drops pattering on the outer edge of the porch a moment, continued, "Well, I'm *surprised* they've nominated Blair."

Mrs. Grant now appeared from within, and also informed "Mr. Grant" of the nominations.

The storm continued, and the General urged the writer to stay until a cessation of its fury. The conversation turned to army experiences, and finally to the writer's adventure with Fowler and Singleton. The General became much interested and listened attentively, at short intervals interposing sharply the single word, "Villains!" At the close, the General asked, —

"And you say you know the names of these men, and where they now live?"

"Yes, sir, — found it all out since the war."

"Well, now you know all about these fellows, what do you propose to do?"

"I don't know what is best; but I am certain that as long as Mrs. Hambrick's interest requires it, nothing will be done with my sanction."

"That is a very sensible conclusion, however much satisfaction would be afforded in seeing the villains punished."

The weeks and months glided swiftly by, and stronger

and stronger grew the desire to revisit the friends and scenes of hardship and danger in the South. Encouraged by the frequent, earnest pleadings which came from that direction, the desire ripened into intention, and the latter was soon after reduced to certainty as to time. Without apprising his Southern friends of his intention to revisit them, the writer perfected his arrangements and left St. Louis, southward bound, on—

February 17, 1870. — The old battle-fields of bloody Mission Ridge, Resaca, and Kenesaw Mountain were passed successively; the familiar scenery surrounding each were objects of great interest to the writer; and in due time he again stood in the improved streets of reconstructed Atlanta. Before venturing further, the writer called upon the officer commanding, Gen. Terry, briefly related his former experience near Decatur, and made known the purpose of his present visit.

The General assured him that there was not the slightest danger to travellers in his department, and of the entire safety in the proposed trip; but it was arranged that if the writer did not report within a few days, a squadron of cavalry should investigate the cause of absence. A jaunt of six miles by rail eastward, and he reached Decatur. *En route* he passed over the battlefield of July 22, 1864; recognized remnants of earthworks, and the unguarded railroad-cut through which the

Confederates swarmed and gained the rear of the Federal lines on that fearful day. As the train emerged from the cut, he looked back to the very spot where he was captured, while on the other side of the railroad was marked the spot where noble McPherson fell. As the visitor alighted at the Decatur depot, he naturally enough glanced in the direction of the recapture. There stood the remnants of the old entrenchments in the distance, and further to the right still stand those *awful woods.* The very sight of them causes an involuntary shudder; danger seems to hover in the very atmosphere about them. The hands instinctively rest upon concealed assurances of ability to repulse the imaginary enemy.

"Do I know where Mrs. Hambrick lives?" repeated the Decatur postmaster, and looking inquiringly at the writer. "Well, yaas; she lives about four mile down that road." (Pointing.)

"Thank you, sir," and the writer departed in the indicated direction. The informer eyed the stranger closely, and *bawled* out after him, —

"They say she *tuck* care of a sick Yankee durin' wartime; be you him?"

(Thunder and lightning! Is it possible?)

Turning partially around, the stranger responded: —

"I know about it, sir. I was down this way, and thought I would deliver a message to her from the gentleman's friends, and try and return to Atlanta *to-night.*"

(I thought I was undoubtedly *dead*—in this neighborhood. Village—everybody knows everything about everybody. How could that old *cogger* suspect me of being a *dead* man?)

> "A village is a hive of glass,
> Where nothing undescried can pass."

After a rapid march over the road he last travelled in an ambulance, he arrived at the gate before the humble residence of Mrs. Hambrick. At the gate stood her boy Isaac, then about eleven years of age, whom the visitor recognized at once.

"Does Mrs. Hambrick live here?"

"Yes, sir," he politely replied.

The writer walked in the gate,—in the door. (There she is!) "Good evening," spoke both together. She eyed the visitor suspiciously, as if half suspecting who he was.

"This is Mrs. Hambrick, I believe?"

She nodded in the affirmative.

"I was requested to call here, madam, by a Mr. Bailey, of St. Louis, and thank you in his name for your many acts of —" "Yes, exactly," said she, interruptingly, "and do you know that I believe *you* are Mr. Bailey himself. You can never conceal that *voice* in this world. Oh! how do you do? how do you do?" and without further ado she fell upon the visitor, and, in the enthusiasm attending the undignified reception, upsetting chairs, demolishing wearing apparel, totally demoralizing the astounded visitor; and, in the attempt to *devour* him, actually created "confusion worse confounded" by knocking off a *wig* the visitor wore, in a vain endeavor to cultivate a luxurious growth of hair.

Well, such a "wooling" and "hazing" need not be envied even as an expression of affection. The "Confederate" onslaught was so sudden and unexpected, and made with such a reckless disregard of personal comfort, that the "Federal" force was completely surprised, speedily overpowered, and ignominiously and unconditionally surrendered.

The successful assault over and the wig feature explained, the whole family mustered and cordially greeted, and comparative calm followed the storm of congratulations and merriment. The "desultory sputtering" which followed, continuing the entire evening until near midnight, was of course directed to the scenes and incidents of '64. Every one had "lots" to say, and all wanted to say it *first*. For more than a mortal hour Mrs. Hambrick's front-room resembled a *cage of magpies*. John, a brother of the hostess, was sent for, and promptly reported. The writer had not forgotten his kindness in placing on his head, while bidding him good-bye in '64, his best hat. After persistent refusals, he finally accepted double the highest estimated value of a new hat, with interest more than compounded from October, 1864. Then John was happy, and taking down his violin, in a manner more spirited than artistic, rattled off a lively but rather indefinite tune, which elicited the applause of the company.

"What's that called, John?" asked the writer.

"'That,'" replied John, straightening up, considerably flushed with his effort and success — "that's called '*Hell broke loose in Georgia.*'"

The visitor now undertook what afforded him rare pleasure, — the distribution of mysterious packages. As they were opened by their recipients, Mrs. Hambrick exclaimed, —

"No, sir, — no, sir, — no more of this, sir; we shall not accept. You have already paid us over and over again for our small services; take this back, sir." "We did not take care of you for *money*," chimed in Mrs. Hambrick's sister, indignantly.

The writer pleasantly but firmly assured them that to imagine that he estimated the value of their services with *money*, was to impugn his motives to such an extent as would make their refusal to accept his small gifts a positive insult. Thereupon, reluctant acceptance was followed by a shower of thanks, from which the bestower of the humble gifts reaped ten times their value.

The next day, the visitor ventured forth to find his other friends in Georgia, promising to return. There was a short jaunt by rail to Covington; *en route*, old

Stone Mountain was passed, — an object of great interest to at least *one* passenger who had seen it before. It looms up now as grandly as when it overlooked contending armies. Now we pass Lithonia, Conyers, — both of which the writer had visited and viewed before, by *starlight*, — and arrive at C.; thence by private conveyance about eight miles, to the plantation near Oak Hill to which they had removed and upon which resided the Freemans. Shortly after dark there was a knocking at the door of the humble log-cabin home, followed by an invitation to "come." The driver of the conveyance and the writer stepped within. All the driver knew was that the writer was seeking "Freeman's" as a suitable place to spend the night. (There sat Mr. and Mrs. Freeman.) A cordial "good-evening" passed all around.

The writer, profiting by the experience with his betraying *voice* at Mrs. Hambrick's, had instructed the driver to request accommodations for the stranger for the night, which he did.

"Certainly, — certainly," responded Mr. F.

The driver warmed himself for a few moments, and returned to Covington. He had hardly closed the door, after bidding us "good-night," before Mr. Freeman said to the visitor, "I reckon I've seen you *before*, sir."

"Possibly."

Mrs. Freeman now exclaimed: "Oh, that's *you*, George! I *knowed* you the minute you came in." Of course, cordial greetings followed; after which the writer inquired for the "girls."

"Where is Siss and her family?"

"They live about a mile down the road, and will be crazy to see you."

Inquiries followed as to Nancy, who was also married, and living a few miles distant; and Betsy? —

"Well, — Betsy; poor Betsy is dead and buried." The writer had not before learned of that recent fact, and every countenance was sad. After supper, "Mig," who had grown from a small boy to a strapping "six-footer," accompanied the visitor to the humble log cabin of young Mr. Freeman and his wife, Siss. A plan — a ruse — a knock — an entry.

"I am mending clocks," said the visitor, disguising his voice; "have you any to mend?"

"No, sir," responded Mr. F. Siss looked at the stranger a moment, and replied, —

"Yes, sir; an' I know you, — I'll never forget them *eyes;* how d'ye, George?" Mig stepped in, in time to join in the hearty laugh which followed. The rather mystified head of the young family, young Mr. F., was then introduced, and the writer said to him, —

"They wouldn't introduce us, sir, when we slept in the same house in '64, when we were in our uniforms."

"No, sir; they were *skeered.* If they had, though, I wouldn't a' gone back to Andersonville again, I tell yer;

I'd gone plumb into your lines with you. I scolded 'em about it when they tol' me of it afterwards."

"What was your duty at the 'pen,' Jake?"

"I was a guardin' Yankee prisoners." (Here's an opportunity.)

"How were our boys treated down there?"

"Oh! like dogs, — *worse* than dogs."

"I'm glad I didn't get there, — bad place, eh?"

"You may thank God you didn't, sir."

"I don't like that *dead-line* I've heard about."

"The dead-line was a mere trap. What I saw there sickened me, sir. Why, the feller who killed a Yankee on the dead-line got a furlough for diligence, — fact, sir. I've seen some of our boys throw crackers and things just outside the dead-line, and then shoot the first poor, starved cuss who reached over for 'em, so he could get a furlough. That was too much for me, sir; I'd rather go without my furlough; that was murder, and nothin' else."

"I'm very glad I concluded not to 'visit' there."

"Between the furloughs and the bloodhounds, the Yanks didn't have much show, I tell yer."

The conversation was prolonged away into the night. The attempt to return to old Mr. Freeman's was met with a decided repulse; so, after we had almost talked ourselves to sleep, there was retirement — sleep — daylight.

When the visitor presented himself for morning salutations, he observed three bright pledges of affection gathered about their young mother, and peering shyly at the stranger. It was not difficult to discover that the little ones had been neatly "fixed up" for the occasion, as they met the writer with bright eyes and sunburnt faces, —

"Shy as the antelope,
Brown as a berry."

"This," said the young mother, illy concealing her pride, and pressing toward the stranger the shrinking form of the eldest, a bright four-year-old, — "this is George Bailey Freeman." The writer's namesake, of course, was made the object of his special admiration. It was not a great while before the visitor secured the confidence of the children, and romped and capered with them as one of *four*.

After breakfast, the entire family escorted the visitor back to the residence of the old folks, where a very pleasant reunion was held, and the incidents of '64 again recalled; after which each of the family were presented with a mysterious package, and "Georgie" received an *extra* recognition, in grateful acknowledgment of the attempt to perpetuate an unworthy name and memory. It afforded the giver, of limited means, much consolation to feel that even his humble gifts were fully appreciated, and constituted *much* to afford relief and secure additional comforts. A trip of a couple of miles, to the residence of *Mrs*. Nancy, including all of the company who were able to go, followed. Meeting — recognition — greeting — merriment.

While here, a group of neighborhood lady callers entered; polite introductions followed.

"A Yankee officer, eh?" repeated one of them, and she entertained the company by relating how several Yankee officers stopped at her house about the time when Sherman "marched to the sea," and slept on her front porch "until near mornin,' when our folks tuck 'em. Ah me!"
"Well," she continued, "it makes me sick to think on't." "Why so?" inquired the writer. "It's a common thing to capture prisoners; I was captured myself." "Aye, Lord; but these were *shot and killed!*" "Indeed? Tell us all about it, please." "Well, you see, 'twas 'bout daylight. There were six on 'em sleepin' on my front porch, and a company of our folks caught 'em, and marched the hull six on 'em off back o' my house, in the woods. I put my head out o' my upper back winder to know what was goin' on. I heered our folks tell 'em, 'Say yer prayers;' and sich pitiful pleadin' I never did hear. I heered 'em say, 'O my poor wife!' 'O my poor mother!' and sich, and they did beg pitiful fur their lives. Then I heered some low prayers, and then, — bang! bang! bang! a few times, — then there was a low moan or two, and all was still. Our folks came back and marched off without even biddin' us good mornin'."

"Do you think their conduct was soldierly or honorable?" inquired the visitor, who had listened throughout with intense interest.

"Honorable! Why, if I hadn't been undressed I should have gone out there an' pleaded for their lives myself; but I knowed it wouldn't a' done no good, nohow. Our folks were all strangers to me, too. Ah me! (with a sigh) we had often heered, afore that, shots scatterin' like — five or six in a bunch — off in the timber, and then we all knew what they meant!" "What became of the bodies of these officers?" asked the writer. "Waal, I was a goin' on to say, they were just barely kivered with leaves, and left jus' so, until they were half eat up by the hogs; then our niggers buried 'em."

"How far from here did this happen, madam?" inquired the writer.

"Why, you can see (stepping to the door and pointing), — that's my house, right over the rise thar; thar's the porch, — you can see, — and right back of the house, in the woods thar, is their graves."

"And you don't know their names or regiments?"

"No, sir; — our folks left nothin' on 'em, — not even all their clothes. I heered 'em call each other 'capt'n,' 'major,' and sich. They didn't pester us, — only slept on the porch, — didn't come in."

After the visiting ladies departed, packages labelled "Nancy" were delivered, and thankfully received. Then we returned to Freeman's. At dinner, the visitor noticed that, contrary to custom, he received his cup of coffee last, and endeavoring to divine a reason for it, he observed that the only spoon on the table was used first for the family, and then turned over to the visitor, and slyly borrowed again by Mrs. F., if required. In order to force an explanation, the writer slyly placed his cup beyond her reach. "Please let me take your spoon a moment," said Mrs. F. The spoon (a coarse leaden one) was passed and returned, which presented a favorable opportunity for the visitor to inquire, —

"Is this a family spoon, Mrs. F.?"

"Well, yes, I reckon it is; we borrow it when we have company." (Possible! so poor as that?)

"Borrow it! Don't you own even one?"

"No, I don't own even one."

Not many weeks after, the Freemans received by express a box of articles from St. Louis, which had been filled by memorandum taken in Georgia, which embraced various useful and ornamental articles, from an abundant supply of large and small *spoons* down to rubber rings for teething babies.

Four days after the arrival at Freeman's, the writer, accompanied by young Mr. and Mrs. F., was conveyed to Covington, where the train was boarded and a hearty good-bye spoken, and soon the visitor reached Decatur, thence to Mrs. Hambrick's, where another welcome awaited him. At the writer's request, old "Aunt Mary," who lived several miles away, had been sent for from Mrs. Hambrick's, and word was awaiting the writer that his faithful old colored friend would be awaiting his arrival at the appointed time and place indicated by the messenger.

The next day, the appointed time, mounted on Mrs. Hambrick's horse, the visitor repaired to the meeting-place, which the faithful woman had walked seven miles to reach. As he approached his old friend, she excitedly raised both hands, loudly exclaiming, —

"Bless de Lord! Bless de Lord! Dat's him! Dat's my boy! Dat's him!" He had hardly dismounted when he was unceremoniously and affectionately enfolded in her dusky arms, and for some moments was unable to extricate himself without seeming very rude; beside, he had no heart to resist her embraces.

She repeatedly assured the writer, who deprecated the necessity of her long walk, that "she'd walk her feet off" to see him, and reminded him that "I always told you dat I thought as much of you as of one o' my own chillen." We sat beside the road, — for we met on the road, — and for nearly an hour talked over the incidents of 1864, when our guns were thundering before Atlanta. She assured the writer that she waited not a moment when he sent for her, and that if his other colored friends knew of his presence, "a whole regiment" of 'em would be there. She was accompanied only by one of her daughters, who had been one of the writer's "pickets" in 1864. They were duly presented with a small roll of "government obligations" as an earnest of gratitude and respect, bade a hearty good-bye, and the old friends parted.

The return to Mrs. Hambrick's was followed by a day of rest and pleasant retrospect, and the pleasant visit was ended.

The facts connected with the attempt to "muster out," as herein related, were established to the satisfaction of the government, and the services and suffering of the writer handsomely recognized by the latter in a substantial manner, the intrinsic value of which is of no consequence compared to the value of the recognition of duty performed in honorable service.

The would-be murderers need have no apprehensions on account of the disturbance of their "blissful ignorance" of the earthly existence of the writer, which will be created by this volume. They will not be tried for their crime before a "jury of their *peers;*" nor has the writer any desire to be tried for a rash act before such "peers;" nor will he follow the beastly example of countenancing, as retaliatory or otherwise, the dark and cowardly arts of the assassin, but will rather exclaim, with the old philosopher who finally succeeded in placing the annoying insects in his power, "Go, poor devils; there's room enough in the world for both thee and me."

Here, properly, this "Private Chapter" draws to a

close. The writer respectfully submits that, from the facts within his limited experiences as herein related, the following conclusions may readily be reached: —

I. That the *whole* South was not in sympathy with the war against the Union; that there was much in the Southern maxim, "The rich man's war, and the poor man's fight;" and that in numberless instances the poor were the mere victims of circumstances which placed them under the control of the aristocracy of wealth, and that while necessity forced action, very many of the actors bore no *real* enmity against the government; that with them it was not a matter of choice, but they were mere *floaters* on the tide of public sentiment, which their standing on the social scale permitted them neither to control nor to stem.

II. That the negroes at the South, as a class, were opposed to the enemies and true to the friends of our government, and were ever ready and willing to render aid and comfort and to make cheerful sacrifices, by day or by night, for our unfortunate straggling "boys in blue," to whose interests and welfare they generally evinced a remarkable degree of fidelity.

III. That localities should not always be condemned because of the unlawful acts of a few; for the vicinity that produces outlaws and fiends to wound, may also be capable of furnishing *angels* to save and comfort the wounded.

IV. That nobility of soul cannot be bound within the narrow confines of sectional prejudices, but, when opportunity is presented, is capable of asserting itself in spite of bitter enmities naturally engendered by civil war.

V. That among the *real* enemies of the government there were at least a few whose *prowling* proclivities found "duties" at the rear, as a pretext to avoid the dangers which threaten *soldiers* at the front — beasts of prey in human form, whose cowardly instincts compelled them to seek only *safe* opportunities to vent their spleen against the government by adding the crime of *murder* to that of treason.

VI. That actual test is the severe but proper criterion by which to determine physical ability to endure exposure and hardship, or to survive the effects of severe bodily injury.

THE END.

www.ingramcontent.com/pod-product-compliance
Lightning Source LLC
Chambersburg PA
CBHW031339230426
43670CB00006B/383